Shockwave Studio
Designing Multimedia for the Web

Shockwave Studio

Designing Multimedia for the Web

Bob Schmitt

Web Review Studio Series

Shockwave Studio: Designing Multimedia for the Web
First Edition
By Bob Schmitt

Published by Songline Studios, Inc. and O'Reilly & Associates, Inc. 101 Morris Street, Sebastopol, CA 95472

Printing History: February 1997: First Edition

Edited by Richard Koman

Cover Illustration by John Hersey

Book Design by Bob Schmitt

Web Review and Web Review Studio are trademarks of Songline Studios, Inc.

This book is printed on acid-free paper with 50% recycled content, 25% post-consumer waste. The publishers are committed to using paper with the highest recycled content available consistent with high quality.

ISBN: 1-56592-231-X

Contents

v

Acknowledgments

Writing a book, I've found, is a more daunting task than I ever thought it could be. Prior to writing this book, I thought — much like most people do — "How hard could it be?" I think it was made doubly hard because of the quick schedule I was on and the fact that I had full-time duties as the creative director of Songline Studios as well as designing and producing this book and its sister book, *GIF Animation Studio.*

With that said, I'd like to thank the following people:

My editor Richard Koman for his work on this book. Without him, the book you hold in your hands would be *far* less readable. I'd also like to thank Richard — and Dale Dougherty — for giving me the opportunity to write this book and for believing I could accomplish the task, and do it well.

Most importantly, I'd like to thank my wife Nancy and daughter Hayley who — because of I've spent every evening and weekend of the last four months writing — thinks her daddy is attached to a computer.

Shockwave has gone through tremendous changes in its first year and I look forward to amazing things in the next year. Additional thanks go to Macromedia for continuing to create fantastic new ways for us artists to practice our craft.

Foreword

By Marc Canter, Canter Technology

So here we are: It's a year after Shockwave shipped, and I'm writing another foreword on the history, reasoning behind, and inspiration that created Shockwave in the first place.

It started off with Jay Fenton and me (who's now also known as Jamie Fenton) creating an animation product named VideoWorks. We needed a way to play back these animations (and sounds) without having to ship the entire tool with the documents.

So I mention to Jay, "Gee, we need a player or something" and he says "Yah, I already took out all the authoring tool code, and here's what I've got left." I went home and called him a few hours later and he says, "OK, I just uploaded it to CompuServe and we've already had 12 people download it!"

"But Jay, maybe we could charge for such a thing!" I say.

"Nay, let's give it away."

And that was that. Years later, untold marketing executives have argued till they were blue in the face that we should charge for our player, but through it all I held strong. "Nope, we're gonna give it away. It'll make Director (the new name of VideoWorks) the industry standard — everyone will use it and we'll make gobs of money selling tools."

That was the original idea behind MacroMind and Director and it lives on today in Shockwave — the VideoWorks player in another form.

We made the industry's second Mac CD-ROM in the summer of 1987 — after Apple did the first — and we stuffed it full of VideoWorks animations, clip art, clip sounds, and some "interactive" applications that included the player. The addition of an interpretive language in VideoWorks by Erik Neumann was another key event in the history of cross-platform players. Jay had done a Tiny Basic version first (for VideoWorks Interactive), but it was Erik and John Thompson (who still works for Macromedia!) who created Lingo in 1987.

The combination of a scripting language with a timeline-oriented scoring system is the reason why Director is today the world's most powerful authoring tool. To see what you're doing and get immediate feedback from changes ... it seems so simple and *right* today, but it wasn't always that good.

I started MacroMind and created Director because I wanted to create these wacky, interactive "experiences" that allowed users to change music, art, and the overall environment. Believe it or not, I didn't do it to make money but to enable the world to create amazing things. We wanted to enable teachers, designers and creative folks. It didn't seem fair that only programmers could do cool digital things.

That's when I first met Jaron Lanier — at a videogame conference. He was demonstrating *Moondust,* this cool roaming-around music environment for the Commodore 64 (before the days of 3D and VR) and I was trying to explain these tools I wanted to build.

I also remember being on stage with Bill Gates — announcing the licensing of our Director player. That was a trip — since I knew he didn't really get the ramifications of building animation into Windows — but I was happy anyway. Microsoft eventually abandoned their plans for building the Director player into Windows, but we were vindicated six years later! Shockwave and Director are one of the few things in the world today that Microsoft hasn't won on!

We also licensed our player to Fujitsu and a bunch of content developers, but it all came down to this: In order to sell cool tools, Macromedia (the new name of MacroMind) needed to keep their player technology up to date, on as many platforms as possible, and out in front of the pack. They've kept that up for seven years now — and they're still leading the pack.

Another Gates Incident happened at a hoity-toity conference in Palm Springs. We were both early to the cocktail party and we starting rapping about cross-platform players; I was arguing that it was the only way to provide developers a comprehensive way of exploiting their assets. Bill's statement was (as he pushed his glasses up back up his nose), "Gee, I don't know — I don't see why you need a cross-platform player. We've got everything you need in Windows."

Well, it turns out that Bill's into cross-platform right now — allowing Microsoft to adapt to the new world of the Internet and beyond. Now not only Gates and Microsoft but the entire world see the ultimate logic of not fighting but joining a revolution. By supporting the cross-platform world, Microsoft ends up winning anyway. As long as all the schmucks on all the non-Microsoft platforms can still communicate with and read and write Windows compatible documents — that's all that matters.

Look at it from an Interactive TV point of view. Do you think that end-users would be happy if they fired up an interactive version of *Laverne and Shirley* or *Melrose Place,* and a message came up on the screen "Sorry your set-top box is not compatible with this software experience, so go out and buy a whatsamacallitt — which we happen to own . . . ?"

Well, that's the essence behind Shockwave — Macromedia is guaranteeing that if you create your content, educational materials, or business messages in Director and play them back with Shockwave, your stuff will work on a wide range of playback platforms for the foreseeable future.

The prospect of a multi-format, multi-platform, multi-standards world means that the only way that creative developers can leverage their work is to develop to a standard such as Shockwave.

By basing all your work on a cross-platform player like Shockwave, a single set of interactive media can be developed as a scalable experience — working just as well on hand-held PDAs, wireless net computers, desktop work machines, or kitchen home things. Game machines, set-top boxes, or car computers are the same sheep in different clothing.

Once a platform has embraced the Shockwave player technology, any and all of what you create *once* can play back over and over again on these disparate platforms. Of course you'll have to create scalable experiences that can adapt to the particular aspects of each of these platforms.

You can't have motion video or rocking sound on a handheld device. You can't display colors on a black and white display. But you can use Lingo to make your content malleable to automatically adapt to the platform.

Just as many Web sites allow viewers to branch between text or graphics mode, content of the future will have three or five different "viewpoints" allowing it to take advantage of the inherent strengths or limitations of each platform. I'm hoping that *all* of these viewpoints — and the switching between them — will be created in Director and played back with Shockwave. In the future Shockwave will be able to stream, play back Java and adapt to ActiveX — in other words, the future is ours.

Enjoy the Shockwave book and remember the immortal words of Woody Guthrie, "Take it easy, but take it." I also like the line we use for *Meet MediaBand,* "The more you click, the weirder it gets."

1

Designing Multimedia for the Web

For the early part of the 1990s, the buzzword in the computing world has been *multimedia*. Last year, that word was replaced with a new catch-phrase, *the Web*. This year, the emergence of a host of new technologies has melded these two concepts together into the indelible future of computing. One of the most exciting of these new technologies is Shockwave.

"A Shockwave Hits the Net." With those words, *Web Review* magazine announced the arrival of Shockwave, Macromedia's technology for viewing multimedia on the Web. Not just any multimedia, their own special kind — the Made-With-Macromedia kind. But Shockwave isn't necessarily a new technology.

For years, Macromedia has led the market in software tools for multimedia developers, and many of the top multimedia CD-ROMs were authored with Macromedia Director. In fact, Director virtually created the field of multimedia by offering an easy-to-learn authoring environment and the ability to create stand-alone applications from Director movies. These applications — known as projectors — can be compiled for any Director-supported platform from the same movie file. Hence Macromedia's slogan, "Author once, play anywhere." This portability allows multimedia authors to create a project on the platform of their choice and to deliver it on other platforms without having to remake the movie.

In late 1995, seeing the Web as a potential new delivery vehicle for multimedia, Macromedia remade their projector technology as a Netscape plug-in which they dubbed "Shockwave." The Shockwave plug-in essentially acts as the projector for the movie file, displaying it right on the Web page.

Read "A Shockwave Hits the Net" by Andrew Leonard in *Web Review* magazine at *http://webreview.com/96/ 02/02/features/shock/*

A Shockwave Hits the Net

In the shocked headline for *Web Review's* article on Shockwave, the tranquil chirping of crickets in the night are interrupted by the supersonic roar of a Shockwave logo speeding by (top). The scene then transitions to a yellow background and a wall of nuclear warning symbols slam together to the sound of a fallout shelter door slamming shut. The headline and buttons appear (middle) and suddenly the nuclear warning symbols begin rapidly flashing in different colors to the deep pulse of unseen heavy machinery (bottom). The four buttons along the bottom of the headline use the Lingo command *gotoNetPage* to send the user to other parts of the story. The *gotoNetPage* command is one of Director's new Net-specific Lingo commands added for use with Shockwave. For more on Net-specific Lingo, see Chapter 9 and Appendix B.

The Shockwave plug-in suddenly made all of the content previously authored with Director available for the Web. With so much content already created and so many multimedia developers familiar with the tools, Shockwave has an enormous head start in bringing high-quality multimedia content to the Web.

When most people talk about Shockwave, they're talking about Director movies running over the Web. Macromedia has also created plug-ins to display content created in their other applications — such as FreeHand, Authorware, Xres, SoundEdit and, most recently, Flash (see sidebar, *A new kid on the block)*. In Macromedia's lexicon, these are all just flavors of Shockwave: the Shockwave Multimedia Player (Director), the Shockwave Graphics Player (FreeHand), the Shockwave Intranet Player (Authorware), and so on. There's no common technology to all these plug-ins; it's just that Macromedia has made the marketing decision to wrap them all up under the same name. While the other forms of Shockwave have their uses, Shockwave for Director is by far the most popular, versatile, and compelling.

Understanding Director

As the name indicates, Director uses a theater or movie metaphor. For example, the elements of your production are called *cast members,* which can be sounds, images, movies, or text — all the things that make up your production. Cast members reside in the *cast* window and are placed on the *stage* to perform. Just like in a Broadway production, the audience can only see the action you put upon the stage.

Once cast members are placed on the stage, they become known as *sprites.* Although sprites are essentially cast members and share all of the cast member's attributes, they can also have unique attributes of their own, such as color, opacity, scaling, visibility, and an associated script. For example, a sprite might have a cast member of a button graphic and a script that takes the user to Frame 2 when the button is clicked. Another sprite might use the same cast member but its script takes the user to Frame 3. Same cast member, different script.

As in Hollywood, Director calls its final output a *movie* (in earlier versions of Director it was called a *filmstrip* and occasionally you'll still hear the term from a long-time user). Each movie is made up of *frames,* just as a film is. Each frame of the movie is made up of separate layers called *channels.* The use of frames and channels are controlled by the user in Director's *score* window.

There are several different types of channels:

- The *tempo channel* controls the movie's speed, measured in frames per second.
- The *palette channel* holds custom palettes for each frame.
- The *transition channel* holds predefined transitions such as fades, wipes and dissolves.
- Two *sound channels* let you play two audio tracks.
- The *script channel* is where you place Lingo scripts, which activate when the movie enters or exits that frame.
- Finally, the score offers 48 *sprite channels,* where you place cast members (mostly graphics) that will appear on the stage.

Just like a Hollywood production, the actions of the movie and the cast are controlled by scripts, written in Lingo, Director's

Puppet commands

Throughout this book, you'll see the use of what are referred to as puppet commands — which also fit the theater metaphor. Lingo's puppet commands, such as *puppet-Sprite* and *puppetSound,* allow a Lingo script to control the actions of a sprite much like a puppeteer pulls the strings of the marionette.

Director's windows

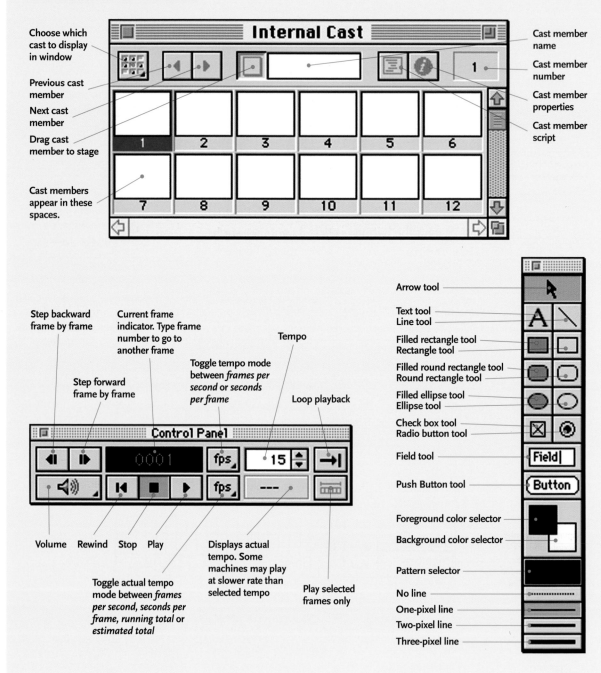

Internal Cast

Choose which cast to display in window

Previous cast member

Next cast member

Drag cast member to stage

Cast members appear in these spaces.

Cast member name

Cast member number

Cast member properties

Cast member script

Step backward frame by frame

Current frame indicator. Type frame number to go to another frame

Step forward frame by frame

Toggle tempo mode between *frames per second* or *seconds per frame*

Tempo

Loop playback

Control Panel

Volume   Rewind   Stop   Play

Toggle actual tempo mode between *frames per second, seconds per frame, running total* or *estimated total*

Displays actual tempo. Some machines may play at slower rate than selected tempo

Play selected frames only

Arrow tool

Text tool
Line tool

Filled rectangle tool
Rectangle tool

Filled round rectangle tool
Round rectangle tool

Filled ellipse tool
Ellipse tool

Check box tool
Radio button tool

Field tool

Push Button tool

Foreground color selector

Background color selector

Pattern selector

No line

One-pixel line

Two-pixel line

Three-pixel line

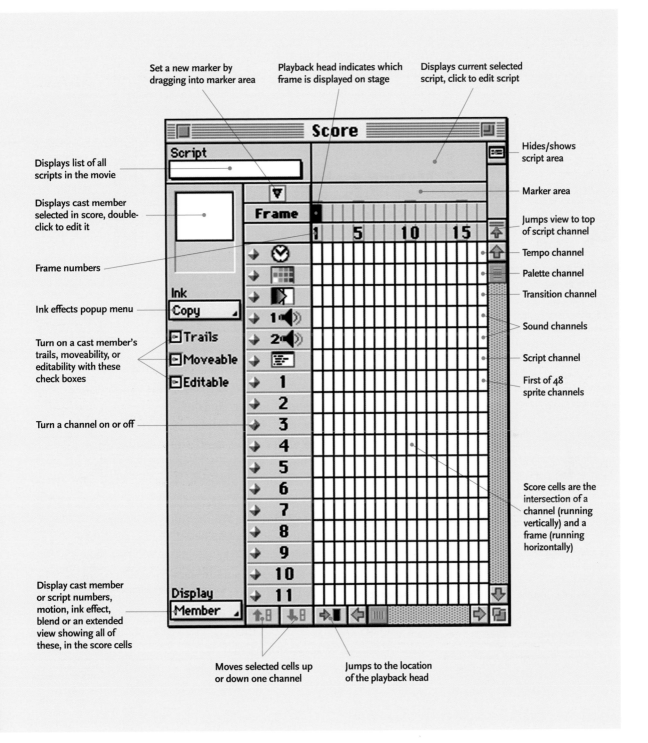

Set a new marker by dragging into marker area

Playback head indicates which frame is displayed on stage

Displays current selected script, click to edit script

Displays list of all scripts in the movie

Displays cast member selected in score, double-click to edit it

Frame numbers

Ink effects popup menu

Turn on a cast member's trails, moveability, or editability with these check boxes

Turn a channel on or off

Display cast member or script numbers, motion, ink effect, blend or an extended view showing all of these, in the score cells

Hides/shows script area

Marker area

Jumps view to top of script channel

Tempo channel

Palette channel

Transition channel

Sound channels

Script channel

First of 48 sprite channels

Score cells are the intersection of a channel (running vertically) and a frame (running horizontally)

Moves selected cells up or down one channel

Jumps to the location of the playback head

Score

Script

Frame

Ink
Copy

☐ Trails
☐ Moveable
☐ Editable

Display
Member

plain-English authoring language. You can use Lingo for simple stage directions — such as navigating from frame to frame or changing cast members on the fly — to programming very complex logic functions. And, while some scripts can become quite complex, the plain-English syntax of Lingo makes understanding and writing scripts well within the reach of the non-programmer. In the following chapters you'll see many examples of Lingo in action.

Making movies Net-friendly

In moving from the world of CD-based multimedia to that of the Web, Macromedia faced a large problem: how to deliver media-rich files over the low bandwidth of the Web. To solve this problem they introduced their Afterburner compression utility.

Afterburning a Director movie provides two very important benefits. A "burned" movie (with a .dcr extension) is a compressed format, offering compression of the type found with programs like Stuffit or PKZip. Depending on the movie, you can achieve compression of anywhere between 40–80%! In addition, this compressed format protects your movies from others opening them in Director and accessing the source Lingo code. (For more information on Afterburning movies, see Appendix A.)

While Afterburning your movies does help reduce the size of the file for download, the more complex issue is learning how to design Director movies that are Net-friendly, which is really what this book is all about. The first thing people bring up when talking about designing for the Web are the many restrictions — such as file size, palette limitations, bandwidth, and page layout. What you rarely hear discussed are the advantages of the Web. Web-based multimedia is a much more dynamic medium than multimedia on a CD, with the ability to link to media all over the world, interact remotely with other programs, and connect to a global audience. Consequently, there is much to learn about designing for this new environment.

The real challenges for multimedia design on the Web are the issues of scalability and extensibility. As Marc Canter

Fried Green Director

Early on in the beta testing process of Shockwave, the file extension was .fgd for "fried green director" to go along with the green frying pan icon (left). This wonderful bit of wackiness, made up by the Shockwave engineers, didn't survive the marketing department, and was subsequently updated to the more corporate extension .dcr (to go along with Director's .dir and .dxr extensions) and its accompanying corporatized icon (right).

Code name: Hopper

Later this year, Macromedia will introduce version 6 of Director, which will include some great new features for Shockwave developers. Here's a look at some of what they're working on:

Streaming Shockwave

Files created with Director 6 will be able to stream over the Web. This will allow developers to deliver much larger movies because the movie will begin playing as the rest of it downloads in the background. (For more information on streaming, see Chapter 11, *Audio Compression with Shockwave.*)

Hybrid Internet applications

The contents of a Shockwave movie will be able to be updated on the fly with a new reusable structure that keeps the content separate from the movie itself.

Browser scripting

Shockwave movies will soon be able to communicate with the browser environment through the use of Javascript and other industry-standard scripting languages. There will also be new Net-specific Lingo commands to control the playback of Shockwave movies and increase interactivity between multiple movies.

Shockwave command recognition

The new version of Director will recognize Net-specific Lingo commands allowing movies to be played and tested from within Director. Currently, Net-specific Lingo has only been recognized by the Shockwave plug-in player, so in order to test a movie it must be played from within a browser.

Another boon for developers is Macromedia's plan to make compressed Shockwave files play with a projector. This will enable multimedia developers publishing on CD to fit much more media on each disk.

Embedded Xtras

With the new version, Xtras will be embeddable in a Shockwave file. This will allow developers to greatly enhance their projects without making the user download and install a separate Xtra.

describes in the foreword, to have lasting value in the rapidly changing world of the Web, multimedia projects need to be easily adaptable for a wide variety of users with varying equipment configurations. Web multimedia must also be extensible, so that new elements can be easily incorporated. These are the challenges that multimedia designers have been grappling with for years, while traditional print designers have not had to worry about them. If you're not familiar with these sorts of issues, this book is meant to help. It will show you many of the strategies, tips, and tricks used by professional multimedia creators who are now working on the Web.

Toward ubiquity

One of the most frequently heard arguments against Shockwave (and Netscape's whole plug-in architecture) is that it requires users to first install the plug-in. Naturally most people creating content for the Web want as many people as possible to be able to see their creations. Many of them will ignore new dynamic technologies and design to the lowest common denominator. Macromedia realized this early on and has taken steps to remedy the situation in the year since Shockwave was introduced.

You can't hang around for long with the folks at Macromedia's San Francisco headquarters without the word "ubiquity" popping up in the conversation. Ubiquity — a word usually associated with the goings on of the Divine Being — has become Macromedia's battle cry and Shockwave their weapon of choice. In order to win the war of multimedia dominance on the Web, Macromedia needs to make Shockwave omnipresent in the Web world. Macromedia not only wants to get Shockwave into the hands of everyone currently using the Web, they want to get Shockwave into the hands of anyone who might ever use the Web in the future. To that end, Macromedia has been busy making deals with the Web's "Big Five" — Netscape, Microsoft, Apple, America Online, and CompuServe.

By the time this book is published, Shockwave will be well on its way to total market ubiquity. They've made deals with Netscape to incorporate Shockwave into their popular browser, not just as a plug-in, but as a "core multimedia content type."

Macromedia has also created an ActiveX component for use with Microsoft's Internet Explorer and have additional plans to incorporate Shockwave into the Windows operating system. "Anywhere Microsoft is, Shockwave will be there too," claimed Marcos Sanchez, former Shockwave product manager.

Macromedia has also made plans with Apple. Shockwave appears in Apple's Internet Connection Kit, which ships with most new Apple computers and as a Cyberdog part for use in Apple's OpenDoc scheme. America Online has also agreed to bundle Shockwave with their browser. And finally, CompuServe has started shipping Shockwave with their online service as well.

All-in-all, Macromedia has high expectations for Shockwave's reach. As David Mendels, Macromedia's director of strategic programs, recently stated, "Our estimates are 30 million enabled browsers by Christmas '96 and 60 million by Christmas '97. Since it is in AOL, Netscape, Microsoft, and the Apple Internet Connection Kit, we will have good coverage of the vast majority of Web browsers worldwide."

All these are significant deals and lead toward a seamless experience for the end user, which makes Shockwave developers very happy.

Shockwave vs. Java

If ubiquity is the goal, why not use Java instead of Shockwave? That's kind of like asking, why not use C or C++? Although they appear to accomplish many of the same goals, there is a dramatic difference in the learning curve required and the mentality of the users of each of these technologies.

Creating Java applets requires serious programming experience. Getting started with Shockwave requires no more skill than it takes to learn any of the popular desktop publishing programs. Unlike the Java language, Lingo uses plain-English commands that are easy to understand and learn. For example, creating a script to take the movie to say, frame 5, is as simple as typing *go to frame 5.* And as you learn more and more Lingo, you will discover more and more that you can do with Director.

The majority of designers either don't have the capacity or the desire to climb the steep learning curve involved in Java

A new kid on the block
Flash mixes the benefits of vector graphics with Shockwave-style interactivity

Recently Macromedia added another flavor of Shockwave to their family of multimedia players by acquiring FutureSplash from FutureWave.

FutureWave, a small San Diego company, released FutureSplash Animator (formerly called Cel Animator) in early 1996 and since then has received nothing but glowing praise from industry pundits. FutureSplash, renamed Macromedia Flash after the purchase, will help fill the gap for designers who want to add interactivity to their pages, but don't need the level of programming Director provides.

Flash is based on FutureWave's Smart Sketch drawing program, which converts freehand drawings into vector curves. Flash takes things a step further by adding timeline-based animation and an easy-to-learn interface for creating interactive buttons. And although Flash can't compete with the level of programming that Director's Lingo language provides, it does offer many very attractive features.

Vector graphics

What makes FutureSplash really stand out is the fact that it's vector-based, much like Macromedia FreeHand files. Vector graphics, depending on their complexity, are much smaller than bitmap files like GIF and JPEG, making file downloads extremely fast. Just as important, Flash files stream, making downloads seem all the quicker, something that has yet to be implemented for Director Shockwave files. Another great feature of vector files is the fact that they are resolution-independent, so you can zoom in for detail without losing any quality or clarity. Although several other plug-ins use vector file formats — Macromedia's Shockwave for Freehand, Adobe's Amber, and Tumbleweed Software's Envoy, to name a few — none of them allow the same level of interactivity and animation that FutureSplash does.

Up, over, and down

Buttons can perform a variety of functions in Flash, from moving to a different frame in the animation or going to a new URL, to moving to a specific frame in a new movie at a new URL. Here again, Flash doesn't provide the high-powered interactivity of programming with Lingo, but it does enough to get you around, and does it nicely.

Another nice touch is that the cursor automatically changes from a pointer to a hand when the user places the mouse over a button. This built-in feature requires no scripting (as is the case with Director) and is consistent across both Windows and Macintosh platforms.

Creating buttons in Flash is as simple as creating three separate pieces of art and merging them, using Flash's button editor. Create one illustration for the button in its normal state, one for when the mouse cursor is over the button, and one for when the mouse button is pressed. Up, over, and down. Once the art is complete, the button can be quickly assembled in Flash's Timeline and Layers window. Flash offers a complete set of drawing tools to create art, including an onion skinning feature that will be a welcome sight to animators.

Flash's Action menu — accessible with a right-mouse click in Windows or a Command-click on a Mac — offers the user some excellent controls over the animation. You can zoom in to see fine detail and zoom back out, all at once or in steps. Also included is a toggle to turn anti-aliasing on or off, rewind, fast-forward, and play the animation, and — most important of all for many users — the ability to toggle looping on and off.

Export capabilities

The unfortunate reality of plug-ins is that not everybody has them all, and many, when they get them, have a difficult time installing them — especially on the Windows side. I'm in the business of collecting and testing plug-ins, and I can't even keep up with them all. What this means for the Web developer is that for every page designed to rely on plug-in technology, they have to create non-plug-in pages. Well, the engineers and designers at FutureWave put in a batch of export options in order to simplify the process.

Need a GIF or JPEG of your animation to use as an imagemap on a non-plug-in page? No problem — Flash exports either. Have to create the non-plug-in page, but can't stand the thought of non-plug-in users missing the cool animations you spent hours toiling on? No problem there either. Flash will export your animation as an animated GIF, Windows AVI, or QuickTime movie. Also, many illustrators and designers have huge investments in learning programs like Macromedia FreeHand and Adobe Illustrator, and might not want to trade in their comfortable programs for the tools in Flash. You can import Illustrator, FreeHand, and AutoCAD DXF files as well as GIFs, JPEGs, and Windows BMP files.

What's missing?

The most obvious thing missing from Flash is sound capability, something that Director handles quite well. What the future holds for Flash is now in the hands of Macromedia. For quite a while now, Shockwave developers have been clamoring for a way to use vector graphics in their Director movies; now that Macromedia has acquired Flash, perhaps a marriage of the two is on the horizon.

As it stands right now, Flash isn't the end-all, be-all of animation on the Web, but it does bring quite a bit to the page, filling a much-needed niche between designers and programers.

programming. The Lingo authoring language, coupled with Director's stage, score, cast and other easy-to-use interface elements make Director the clear choice for the designer.

Using this book

There are several things that you should be aware of before getting started with the rest of this book.

The intention of this book is not to be the definitive guide to Lingo or Director, but it's not a book for dummies either. We'll be moving rather quickly into real-world examples and covering only briefly many of the basic concepts of Lingo and workings of Director. Although everything you need to understand the concepts discussed in the book are there, if you're not experienced with Director you'll want to keep the manuals or an in-depth Director or Lingo book at hand.

Using the CD

As you read through the book, you'll want to explore the contents of the CD-ROM. I've included Lingo source code for most of the samples in the book and you will get a lot out of opening these files and examining them as you read. Although a great deal of the movies are explained in the book, there are many things in each movie I've left for you to discover. I personally find that one of the best ways to learn Director is to dissect a movie's source code and to see just how it was put together. For more detailed information about the CD, see Appendix D.

2

Animating
with Shockwave

To learn more about
GIF animation techniques,
be sure to get your copy
of the companion book to
Shockwave Studio:
*GIF Animation Studio:
Animating Your Web Site*
by Richard Koman,
ISBN #1-56592-230-1

Until recently, Web pages were static — filled with text and still images. The only way a designer could manage a little dynamic movement was with *server push*, a technique that — depending on your bandwidth — would either play at the equivalent of a very slow slide show or blow by so quickly you couldn't even see it. That all changed last year when GIF animation burst into popular use. Now it seems every page has some sort of dancing, jiggling, pulsating object. Some nicely done, others not so nice. GIF animation has many advantages, including ease of use, cheap/free authoring software, and streaming (it displays as it downloads instead of waiting until it is completely downloaded before starting). There's no need for users to download a plug-in or helper application, and no need for designers to configure the server.

Shockwave offers none of these advantages, but it does offer many more attractive features, including the ability to bring full CD-ROM-quality multimedia to the Web page. Shockwave provides an authoring language (Lingo) that enables virtually unlimited interactivity, complex logic functions, branching, and rollover effects. Shockwave's Afterburner compression scheme compresses graphics as small or smaller than GIF compression. Shockwave reuses cast members within an animation, enabling Shockwave movies to have much smaller file sizes than equivalent GIF animations (see sidebar, "The Shockwave Difference"). Shockwave also allows the use of sound, essential to creating a compelling experience.

Figure 2-1. The Director icon animation. On the CD open the file *tutorial/source/timeline.dir* to see it in action.

Throughout this book, you'll see there are many ways to accomplish an effect. The one you choose will depend on the specific characteristics of your project. In this chapter we'll build the animation you see depicted across the top of this spread (Figure 2-1). This animation transitions from the Director icon to a filmstrip, the filmstrip plays for a few seconds, and then transitions back to the Director icon.

We'll discuss three basic methods in this chapter:

- Timeline-based animation
- Film loops
- Lingo-based animation

Creating a timeline-based animation

The most basic form of animation in Shockwave is timeline-based. Simply put, this is a series of graphics placed linearly in Director's score window. It is similar to the old flip-book-style animations where one image follows another, from beginning to end. Timeline-based animations can be set to run once, from the first frame to the last frame, or set to loop over and over again.

The first step in creating a timeline-based animation is to import your images into the cast. Open the cast window by selecting **Window/Cast** (see Figure 2-2). Highlight the first cast space by clicking on it, then select **File/Import** to open the *Import Files* dialog box (Figure 2-3). In the top part of the window, find the *tutorial/cast* folder on your CD-ROM and select *D01.pic,*

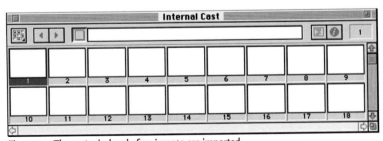

Figure 2-2. The cast window before images are imported.

Figure 2-3. The *Import Files* dialog box.

Director tip

When creating your graphics, be sure to save them in a separate folder. Call it something like *Cast*. Also, name them alphabetically or numerically. This allows you to click on the *Add All* button to import all the images in the folder, which will save you a lot of time and clicking. Just be sure there are no graphics in the directory that you don't need in your cast, as they will be added as well. By naming them alphabetically or numerically, all the graphics will be added to the cast in the correct order of the animation. That's something that will come in handy in later steps.

the first graphic in the animation. Click on the *Add* button to add it to the list in the bottom half of the window. If your folder contains only the images you wish to import, as in this case, click *Add All*. If this isn't the case, you'll have to add each image individually.

Once your list is complete, click *Import*. This brings up the *Image Options* dialog box for the first cast member in the list (Figure 2-4). Here you can select the color depth and palette for

Figure 2-4. The *Image Options* dialog box.

The Shockwave difference

World-renowned illustrator Henrik Drescher created this animation called *Hare Krishna Cyclotron* (Figure 2-a). He chose to use GIF animation as the format for the animation, which resulted in a final file size of just over 123K. I wanted to see what the result would be if we used the same art and created the animation in Shockwave. First let's take a look at the frames of the existing GIF animation as shown in Figure 2-b. As you can see, the GIF animation is made up of 26 individual GIFs. Now let's look at the cast window of the same animation as created in Director (Figure 2-c). The animation actually uses only 18 unique images, the other eight, used in the GIF animation, are repeats. Because of Director's superior cast and score structure, those eight repeats are reused in the score of the Shockwave movie rather than repeated in the cast. This arrangement allows the designer to reuse cast members endlessly with little to no addition in the file size of the final animation. In fact, the final size of our Shockwave movie is just under 84K, a full 40K less than the GIF animation.

To further illustrate this point, I wanted to see what would happen to the respective file sizes of the GIF animation and the

Hare Krishna Cyclotron by Henrik Drescher.

Frames					
26 frames	Length: 5.55 s	Size: 775x550			Loop: forever
Name	Size	Position	Disp.	Delay	Transp.
Frame 1	195x142	(286; 222)	N	–	–
Frame 2	59x113	(281; 427)	N	75	–
Frame 3	195x142	(286; 222)	N	–	–
Frame 4	59x113	(281; 427)	N	40	–
Frame 5	195x142	(286; 222)	N	–	–
Frame 6	89x113	(281; 427)	N	40	–
Frame 7	195x142	(286; 222)	N	–	–
Frame 8	142x99	(410; 433)	N	40	–
Frame 9	195x142	(286; 222)	N	–	–
Frame 10	100x142	(564; 347)	N	40	–
Frame 11	195x142	(286; 222)	N	–	–
Frame 12	87x149	(655; 235)	N	40	–
Frame 13	195x142	(286; 222)	N	–	–
Frame 14	120x177	(606; 60)	N	40	–
Frame 15	195x142	(286; 222)	N	–	–
Frame 16	133x184	(479; 6)	N	40	–
Frame 17	195x142	(286; 222)	N	–	–
Frame 18	107x177	(358; 5)	N	40	–
Frame 19	195x142	(286; 222)	N	–	–
Frame 20	168x170	(184; 12)	N	40	–
Frame 21	195x142	(286; 222)	N	–	–
Frame 22	137x163	(47; 83)	N	40	–
Frame 23	195x142	(286; 222)	N	–	–
Frame 24	185x163	(15; 234)	N	40	–
Frame 25	195x142	(286; 222)	N	–	–
Frame 26	157x135	(117; 378)	N	40	–

Figure 2-b. The frames for the *Cyclotron* GIF animation as shown in the popular Macintosh program, GIFBuilder.

Figure 2-a. The *Hare Krishna Cyclotron* animation.

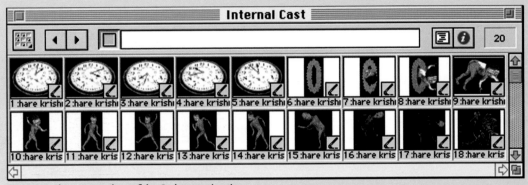

Figure 2-c. The cast members of the *Cyclotron* animation.

Shockwave movie if I reversed the sequence of the animation and added it to the end of the existing animation. So, after the baby leaves the womb, grows to manhood and crumbles into dust, the animation will reverse going from the skeleton, to manhood and finally back into the womb. When I constructed this in GIF animation format, the final animation contained 51 layers of GIFs, and the file size rose to a whopping 241K! I did the same thing with the Shockwave movie, duplicating frames two through 14 and reversing the sequence (Figure 2-d). And the result? The file size rose a mere 101 bytes, one-tenth of a kilobyte. This is a significant advantage over GIF animation, especially with complex or large animations such as this.

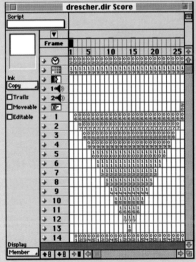

Figure 2-d. The score of the animation coming and going.

the image. (For a discussion of palettes and color depth issues, see Chapter 8, *Avoiding Problems with Palettes.*) Be sure to select the *Same Settings for Remaining Images* checkbox. This applies these settings to all the graphics in the list.

Next, open the score window by selecting **Window/ Score.** The score is the timeline of the movie, a grid of cells consisting of frames (running horizontally) and channels (running vertically). Frames act like the individual frames of a motion picture: each frame can contain different elements in different positions. Channels control attributes of the movie, such as tempo, sound, transitions, palette, etc. The score window is described in more detail in Chapter 1, *Designing Multimedia for the Web.*

There are several ways to set up your animation but probably the easiest is the *Cast to Time* feature. In the score window, select the first frame of the first sprite channel by clicking it once (the square will turn dark; see Figure 2-5). Next, in the cast window, select all the images of your animation (click once on the first image, hold down the Shift key, and click on the last image; see Figure 2-6).

Then choose **Modify/Cast to Time.** The cast members appear sequentially in sprite channel 1 in the score (see Figure 2-7) and are centered on the stage. At this point you can check the progress of your animation by selecting **Control/Play.**

Note that we only have images for the first half of the animation. That's because we'll reuse these images to create the second half. First we need to add a few more frames to the animation. We'll accomplish this quickly and easily by duplicating frames in the score window.

Select frames 8 and 9. Then, while holding down the Option key (the Alt key in Windows), drag frames 8 and 9 to frames 10 and 11 (see Figure 2-8). Holding down Option (or Alt) copies frame 8 and 9 to frames 10 and 11. Repeat this process three more times, filling in frames 12 through 17.

Now, to animate the transition from the filmstrip to the Director icon, we need to reverse the order of frames 1–8 in frames 18–25. Start by selecting frames 1–8. Then, holding the

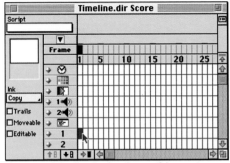

Figure 2-5. Selecting the first frame of the movie.

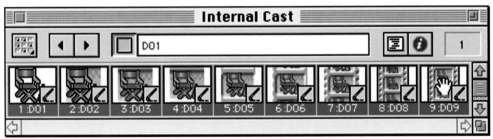

Figure 2-6. Selecting all the members in the cast window.

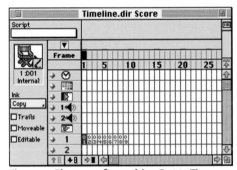

Figure 2-7. The score after applying *Cast to Time*.

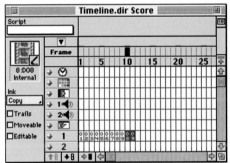

Figure 2-8. Copying frames 8–9 to frames 10–11.

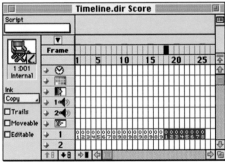

Figure 2-9. Copying frames 1–8 to frames 18–25.

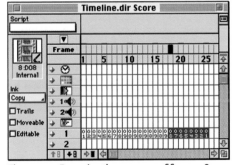

Figure 2-10. Reversing the sequence of frames 18–25.

Animating with Shockwave

Figure 2-11. The *Tempo* dialog box. If you're familiar with Director's *Wait* settings, don't expect to use them in Shockwave: they've all been disabled.

Option (or Alt) key down, drag frames 1–8 to frames 18–25 to copy them (Figure 2-9). With frames 18–25 still selected, select **Modify/Reverse Sequence** (Figure 2-10). Play the completed animation to check your work.

Changing the tempo

At this point, the animation is moving too quickly at the default 30 frames per second (fps), so we'll need to slow it down a bit. Double-click in frame 1 of the tempo channel in the score window to bring up the *Tempo* dialog box (see Figure 2-11). Select the *Tempo* radio button, if it's not already selected, and change the frame rate by moving the slider or clicking on the arrows. The tempo you choose will be a matter of personal preference; experiment with different settings until you find a setting you like. I chose a rate of 15 fps. Keep in mind that playing back over the Web as a Shockwave movie, the actual fps will be dependent on the speed of each viewer's individual computer. Although your movie may play slower on some machines, it will never go faster than the optimal setting you choose here.

Looping

Finally, we'll write a simple Lingo script to make this timeline-based animation loop continuously.

In the score window, click on the script channel in the final frame of the animation (frame 25). Now go to the *Script* pop-up menu in the upper-left corner of the score window and select *New Script*. This brings up the *Score Script* window with an empty

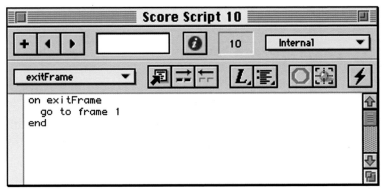

Figure 2-12. The *exitFrame* handler.

exitFrame handler (Figure 2-12). On the line between *on exitFrame* and *end* type *go to frame 1* (you can shorten this to *go frame 1* or even *go 1*). Close the window and play the completed animation. To test that the looping script is working, be sure **Loop Playback** is deselected under the **Control** menu.

There you have it: a simple timeline-based animation of the Director icon transitioning into a filmstrip and back again. All that's left to do is burn your movie, add it to your Web page, and upload it to your server. For instructions on how to do this, see Appendix A.

Creating a film loop

Now that we've completed our timeline-based animation, let's turn it into a *film loop.* A powerful tool in Director, a film loop is simply an animated sequence, created like any other timeline-based animation, but represented as a single sprite rather than being composed of multiple sprites spread across multiple frames as in the timeline-based animation. This is especially useful if you have animations of varying lengths playing on the stage simultaneously. It can also save a lot of score space. Let's use our sample from the last section and make a film loop. In this tutorial, we'll learn how to create a film loop, use it in the score, and write a Lingo script that runs the animation.

The first step is to highlight in the score all of the frames to be included in the film loop (Figure 2-13). Make sure you have the cast window open, then simply drag the frames from the

The *exitFrame* handler

An *exitFrame* handler responds to one of Director's built-in events that commonly occur during movie play. *MouseUp, mouseDown, startMovie,* and *enterFrame* are other examples of these built-in events. When the movie exits a frame, Director sends out the *exitFrame* message, which activates the handler.

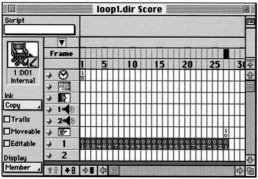

Figure 2-13. Highlighting frames for the film loop.

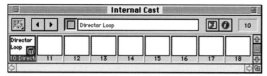

Figure 2-14. Dragging the highlighted frames to the cast window creates the film loop.

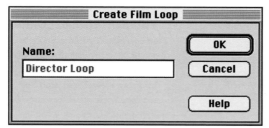

Figure 2-15. Name the film loop in the *Create Film Loop* dialog box.

Director tip

After making a film loop, be sure not to delete any of the cast members that were used. The film loop does not contain any of the actual cast members, it is merely a recording of the score information that defines the film loop. The cast members must be present in the movie for the film loop to work.

See it in action

To see this next variation in action, play the movie *tutorial/source/loop2.dir* in Director. The movie *tutorial/source/loop1.dir* shows the stuttering effect that happens when the *rollover* is not trapped as described in the "Making it interactive" section.

score window into an empty space in the cast window (Figure 2-14). This brings up the *Create Film Loop* dialog box (Figure 2-15). Name the film loop *Director Loop,* and click *OK.*

To use your new film loop, first delete the timeline-based animation from the score: you won't be needing it anymore. Next, drag the film loop you just created from the cast window to sprite channel 1 of frame 1 in the score.

In this example the film loop occupies only one frame; in other movies a film loop might span several frames. In either case, the movie ends when it has played through the frames. With only one frame, the movie would end before the film loop has even started. In order to keep the film loop moving, we need to write a Lingo script that loops the movie in frame 1.

Start by double-clicking in the script channel of frame 1. This brings up an empty *Score Script* window. On the line after *on exitFrame,* type *go to the frame* and close the *Score Script* window. You can now check your film loop by selecting **Control/Play.**

Making it interactive

Finally, let's make the animation interactive by making it move only when the mouse is over it. We'll use a simple Lingo script to switch from a static image when the mouse isn't over the sprite to the film loop when it is over the sprite.

We'll start out with the static image. Using our work-in-progress, we'll quickly switch a static image for the film loop using the **Edit/Exchange Cast Members** menu command. Select the film loop in sprite channel 1 of frame 1. Next, open the cast window and select cast member 1: the Director icon graphic. Then go to **Edit/Exchange Cast Members.** This switches the cast member in the score for the one selected in the cast. Now all that's left is to add a few lines of Lingo to the *exitFrame* script created previously.

We want to create a *rollover* effect, in which the animation only runs when the mouse is over the sprite. Ordinarily creating a rollover in Director is as simple as using a script similar to the one shown in Figure 2-16. In that *exitFrame* handler, the script first checks to see if the mouse is over the sprite in channel 1 *(rollover(1))*. If so, it changes the cast number of sprite 1 to the cast number of a different sprite, then updates the stage to show the change. If the mouse isn't over the sprite, the script swaps the cast numbers back again. We'll go through rollovers in detail in Chapter 3.

While this technique is fine for swapping static images, it causes a problem with film loops. The problem is that every time the *exitFrame* handler is repeated (15 times per second in our example) the cast of sprite 1 is reset to the *DirectorLoop* cast member, over and over again. This causes a nasty stuttering effect. To correct for this, we need to *trap* the state of the rollover. To do this we use a *variable* (to learn more about variables, see Chapter 4, *The Power of Variables)*. By using a variable, we can tell the movie whether we want it to switch to the film loop or not simply by changing the value in the variable. Here's how it works:

First we'll create a new movie script. If the *Score Script* window isn't open already, open it by double-clicking the score channel in frame 1 of the score. This brings up the *exitFrame* handler script we created earlier. To create the new movie script, simply click the + symbol in the top-left corner of the *Score Script* window. In this new *Movie Script* window, enter the script shown in Figure 2-17. This script, activated on the start of the movie, simply creates a global

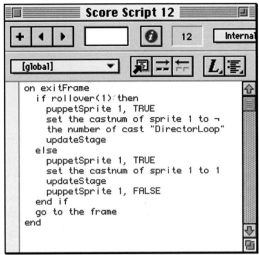

Figure 2-16. A typical *rollover* script.

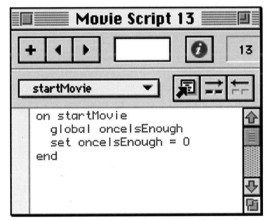

Figure 2-17. The *startMovie* handler is triggered when the movie starts, creating the *onceIsEnough* variable.

About *if...then*

The *if...then* statement is one of the most often-used Lingo structures. In an *if...then* statement, Lingo checks to see if the expression following the word *if* is true. If it is true, Lingo executes the statements following the word *then*. If false, Lingo skips the rest of the statements in the *if...then* structure (the *if...then* structure ends with a matching *end if* statement) and moves on to any additional lines of code in the script. *If...then* structures can also contain an *else* statement, which contains elements that are executed if the *if...then* portion of the statement is false.

Director tip

To move back in the script window, simply click on the left arrow at the top-left side of the window.

variable that we've named *onceIsEnough*. It then sets the value for this variable to 0. This initial value is used later in the *exitFrame* script. Now let's move back to the *exitFrame* handler we made earlier.

Back in the *exitFrame* handler, we'll make the changes to the script, adding the lines before the *go to the frame* command as shown in Figure 2-18. This script is similar to the first rollover script shown in Figure 2-16, but with one important difference. In this new script we first declare the global variable *onceIsEnough*, **Ⓐ** which at this point is equal to 0. Next we have two *if...then* statements, which check for two different states of *onceIsEnough*. The first state (where *onceIsEnough* = 0) indicates that the mouse has not rolled over sprite 1. The second state (where *onceIsEnough* = 1) indicates that the mouse is over sprite 1.

If the value of *onceIsEnough* is 0, **Ⓑ** the script checks to see if the mouse is over sprite 1. **Ⓒ** If it is, the commands after the word *then* are executed. These commands are the same as in the first rollover script (Figure 2-16): the *puppetSprite* command **Ⓓ** puts the sprite under the control of Lingo, then the static cast member is swapped for the film loop cast member **Ⓔ** and the stage is updated to show the change. **Ⓕ**

After this, *onceIsEnough* is set to 1. **Ⓖ** This causes the script to ignore the first *if...then* statement on subsequent repeats of the handler, and to go directly to the second *if...then* statement. **Ⓗ** This second statement checks to see if the mouse is over sprite 1, **Ⓘ** and if it's not, the script changes the film loop back to the static image of the Director icon (cast member number 1), **Ⓙ** and the variable *onceIsEnough* is set back to 0. **Ⓚ**

Animating with Lingo

One of the drawbacks of using a film loop to animate is that a film loop can't have a script attached to it, thus the user can't click on it. If you need to animate in a single frame of a movie and want the animation to be clickable, try animating with Lingo. With a simple Lingo script you can step through a series of cast members, just as a film loop does, and maintain the ability to have the user interact with it. In this example, we'll re-create the animation from the last section using Lingo instead of a film loop. This time the user will have to click on the image to see the animation.

See it in action

To see this variation in action, play the movie *tutorial/source/lingo.dir* in Director.

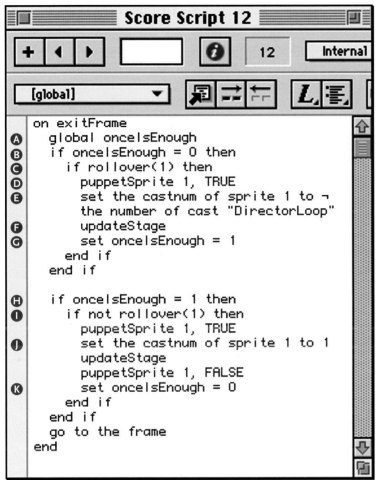

Figure 2-18. This *exitFrame* handler avoids the stuttering effect.

```
on exitFrame
  global onceIsEnough
  if onceIsEnough = 0 then
    if rollover(1) then
      puppetSprite 1, TRUE
      set the castnum of sprite 1 to ¬
      the number of cast "DirectorLoop"
      updateStage
      set onceIsEnough = 1
    end if
  end if

  if onceIsEnough = 1 then
    if not rollover(1) then
      puppetSprite 1, TRUE
      set the castnum of sprite 1 to 1
      updateStage
      puppetSprite 1, FALSE
      set onceIsEnough = 0
    end if
  end if
  go to the frame
end
```

We'll use the same setup from the last section. Remember, we have the Director icon (the first cast member) in sprite channel 1 and an *exitFrame* handler in the *Score Script* channel with a *go to the frame* statement. Now we'll attach a *mouseUp* handler to sprite 1 (the Director icon). This script will define what happens when the user clicks on the sprite.

Let's look at the Lingo we'll use to accomplish this animation.

The *mouseUp* script (Figure 2-19), attached to the Director icon in sprite channel 1, has one purpose: to call a custom handler called *animateMe* when the sprite is clicked on.

The *animateMe* script (Figure 2-20) first creates a local variable called *loopCount* and sets its initial value to 5.  **A** This variable is used later in the script.

Next it enters into a repeat loop. **B** This loop will create the first part of the animation — the Director icon transitioning into the film strip. This loop repeats 9 times with the variable *x* assigned the numbers 1 through 9. *X* will equal 1 on the first iteration of the loop, 2 on the next loop and so on, until *x* equals 9.

On each successive iteration of this loop, the cast number of sprite 1 is set to equal the number contained in the variable *x*. **C** This marches through the animation from cast member 1 through 9. In order to control the speed of the animation, we set up another repeat loop at the end of each loop in this sequence. First, Lingo's timer is started, **D** and then the *repeat* loop starts, doing nothing but delaying the movie until the timer has passed 4 ticks. **E**

After the final iteration of the *repeat with* loop, the script immediately moves on to the next segment of the animation.

This portion creates the illusion of the film strip moving. Here we use a *repeat* loop with the *loopCount* variable created earlier. **F** This loop continues to repeat itself for as long as the value contained in *loopCount* is greater than 0. Within this loop, sprite 1 is changed to cast member 8, **G** and after a 4-tick delay, **H** it's then changed to cast member 9. **I** After another short delay **J** and before the loop is repeated, the script subtracts 1 from *loopCount*. **K** This has the effect of making this loop repeat five times. Each time through the loop, *loopCount* equals 1 less than the time before, until it finally equals 0, and the script exits this repeat loop and moves to the last portion of the animation.

The last portion of the *animateMe* script reverses the sequence of the first portion of the script, transitioning the filmstrip back into the Director icon. This is again done with a local variable *x*, which is set to equal 9. **L** A *repeat* loop runs until *x* equals 0. **M** Each time through the loop, sprite 1 is set to equal whatever cast member number is contained in the variable *x*. **N** After this, 1 is subtracted from the number contained in *x*. **O** This creates a countdown from 9 to 1, effectively reversing through the list of cast members.

Figure 2-19. The *mouseUp* script.

Shockwave Studio

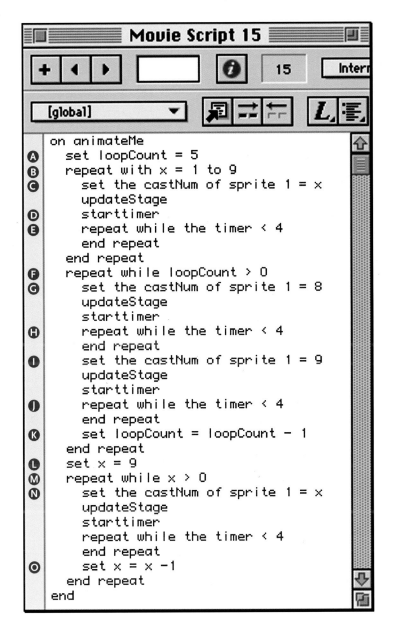

```
Movie Script 15                    15    Interr
[global]

   on animateMe
A    set loopCount = 5
B    repeat with x = 1 to 9
C      set the castNum of sprite 1 = x
       updateStage
D      starttimer
E      repeat while the timer < 4
       end repeat
     end repeat
F    repeat while loopCount > 0
G      set the castNum of sprite 1 = 8
       updateStage
       starttimer
H      repeat while the timer < 4
       end repeat
I      set the castNum of sprite 1 = 9
       updateStage
       starttimer
J      repeat while the timer < 4
       end repeat
K      set loopCount = loopCount - 1
     end repeat
L    set x = 9
M    repeat while x > 0
N      set the castNum of sprite 1 = x
       updateStage
       starttimer
       repeat while the timer < 4
       end repeat
O      set x = x -1
     end repeat
   end
```

Figure 2-20. The *animateMe* script. The entire script re-creates the simple animation that we created very easily as a timeline-based animation and film loop. Animating with Lingo allows us to animate in a single frame and gives us the ability to make it interactive — in this case by triggering the animation when the user clicks on the Director icon.

Of course there are many variations to this basic formula — each project is unique — and some Lingo animations can become quite complex as seen in the sidebar, "Exploring the Planet's Orbiter." In the rest of the book we'll focus on using Lingo to create more sophisticated interactive experiences in Director and Shockwave.

Exploring The Planet's Orbiter

```
ON AnimatePlanets

  -- PLANET WITH ORBITERS
  GLOBAL PurpleOrbit, YellowOrbit, PurpleSprite, YellowSprite, PurpleBackMost, TheCast
  GLOBAL YellowBackMost, PurpleCos, PurpleSin, YellowCos, YellowSin, PurpleX, PurpleY
  GLOBAL YellowX, YellowY, XPos, YPos, TheSide

  SET PurpleOrbit = PurpleOrbit + 0.0175
  IF NOT PurpleBackMost THEN
   IF PurpleOrbit > 3.15 THEN
     -- Purple BackMost
     SET PurpleBackMost = TRUE
     SET THE LocH OF Sprite 17 TO -200
     SET PurpleSprite = 9
   END IF
  ELSE IF PurpleOrbit > 6.2832 THEN
   -- Purple ForeMost
   SET PurpleBackMost = FALSE
   SET PurpleOrbit = 0
   SET THE LocH OF Sprite 9 TO -200
   SET PurpleSprite = 17
  END IF

  SET PurpleCos = Cos(PurpleOrbit)
  SET PurpleSin = Sin(PurpleOrbit)
  SET PurpleX = (70 * PurpleCos)
  SET PurpleY = (20 * PurpleSin)
  SET PurpleXX = Integer((((PurpleX * 2) + 200) * 10000) / 10000)
  SET TheSide = (10000*PurpleXX) MOD 10000
  SET PurpleXX = ((10000*PurpleXX) - TheSide) / 10000
  SET PurpleYY = Integer((((PurpleY * 2) + 200) * 10000) / 10000)
  SET TheSide = (10000*PurpleYY) MOD 10000
  SET PurpleYY = ((10000*PurpleYY) - TheSide) / 10000
  SET XPos = PurpleXX MOD 2
  SET YPos = PurpleYY MOD 2
  SET TheCast = (2 * Xpos) + YPos

  -- Purple Outline:

  SET THE CastNum OF Sprite 4 TO (25 + TheCast)

  SET THE LocH OF Sprite 4 TO (PurpleXX/2) - 20
  SET THE LocV OF Sprite 4 TO (PurpleYY/2) - 65

  -- Purple Moon:

  SET THE CastNum OF Sprite PurpleSprite TO 35 + TheCast

  SET THE LocH OF Sprite PurpleSprite TO (PurpleXX/2) - 20
  SET THE LocV OF Sprite PurpleSprite TO (PurpleYY/2) - 65

  SET YellowOrbit = YellowOrbit + 0.0262
  IF NOT YellowBackMost THEN
   IF YellowOrbit > 3.1440 THEN
     -- Yellow BackMost
     SET YellowBackMost = TRUE
     SET THE LocH OF Sprite 16 TO -200
     SET YellowSprite = 10
   END IF
  ELSE IF YellowOrbit >= 6.2832 THEN
   -- Yellow ForeMost
   SET YellowBackMost = FALSE
   SET YellowOrbit = 0
   SET THE LocH OF Sprite 10 TO -200
   SET YellowSprite = 16
  END IF

  SET YellowCos = Cos(YellowOrbit)
  SET YellowSin = Sin(YellowOrbit)
  SET YellowX = (54 * YellowCos)
  SET YellowY = (14 * YellowSin)
  SET YellowXX = Integer((((YellowX * 2) + 200) * 10000) / 10000)
  SET TheSide = (10000*YellowXX) MOD 10000
  SET YellowXX = ((10000*YellowXX) - TheSide) / 10000
  SET YellowYY = Integer((((YellowY * 2) + 200) * 10000) / 10000)
  SET TheSide = (10000*YellowYY) MOD 10000
  SET YellowYY = ((10000*YellowYY) - TheSide) / 10000
  SET XPos = YellowXX MOD 2
  SET YPos = YellowYY MOD 2
  SET TheCast = (2 * Xpos) + YPos

  -- Yellows Outline:
  SET THE CastNum OF Sprite 3 TO (21 + TheCast)
  SET THE LocH OF Sprite 3 TO (YellowXX/2) - 20
  SET THE LocV OF Sprite 3 TO (YellowYY/2) - 66

  -- Yellow Moon:
  SET THE CastNum OF Sprite YellowSprite TO 31 + TheCast
  SET THE LocH OF Sprite YellowSprite TO (YellowXX/2) - 20
  SET THE LocV OF Sprite YellowSprite TO (YellowYY/2) - 66

  UpdateStage

END
```

**Figure 2-e. This script from The Planet's *Orbiter*
shows how complex animating with Lingo can get.**

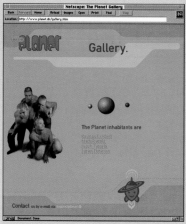

Figure 2-f. The Planet's Gallery page.

In this chapter we've shown some basic methods of animating in Shockwave, including how to animate using Lingo. While our example of controlling a single sprite in Lingo was simple, there are more complex ways of controlling animations with Lingo. A good example is the Orbiter project (Figure 2-e).

We put this sample on the disk for those intrepid souls who wish to wade into a more complex example of Lingo animation (open *source/orbiter.dir* on your CD). The designers at The Planet (*http://www.planet.dk/*) created the animation of two smaller spheres orbiting a larger sphere that appears on their gallery page (Figure 2-f). They used the *cos* and *sin* Lingo functions to create an excellent example of the Lingo language's complex logic and math functions.

3

Creating
Rollover Effects

One of the biggest problems with the Web is the lack of user feedback. Is something happening? Is this a clickable button or just a piece of art? Rollover effects are an excellent way to improve the Web experience by giving users clues about their interaction with the site. For years, rollover effects have been used in multimedia projects to enhance communication with the user, typically by highlighting graphics with a glow or color change. Creatively used, though, rollovers can do more than just highlight buttons. You can use them to create interesting and creative effects, some of which we'll look at in this chapter.

Figure 3-1.

The basic rollover

The term *rollover* refers to the mouse rolling over an element. That is, something happens when the cursor is placed over the graphic and then returns to the original state when the cursor leaves the graphic. Figure 3-1 shows a basic rollover: a red button turns green when the mouse is placed over it and returns to red when the mouse moves off the graphic.

In Shockwave, the basic rollover effect is created with the Lingo command *rollover*. This command is usually placed in an *exitFrame, enterFrame,* or *idle* handler. The rule of thumb is that it needs to be in a place the movie checks constantly. Figure 3-2 shows a typical *rollover* handler. This is a simple script that changes the red button to green when the mouse is over it.

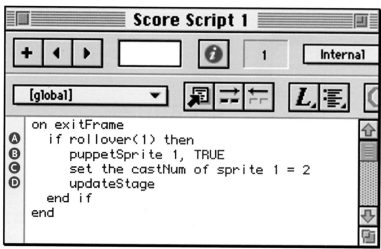

Figure 3-2. A basic *rollover* script.

```
on exitFrame
    if rollover(1) then
        puppetSprite 1, TRUE
        set the castNum of sprite 1 = 2
        updateStage
    end if
end
```

The first line of this script Ⓐ checks to see if the mouse is over the sprite contained in sprite channel 1. This channel contains the graphic of the button in its "off" state (when the cursor is not over it). The next line Ⓑ puts this sprite under the control of Lingo. Next, the script sets the cast number of the sprite in channel 1 to 2. Ⓒ Cast member 2 is the graphic for the button in its "on" state (when the cursor is over the graphic.) Finally, the stage is updated to show the change. Ⓓ

While rollover buttons are a common use of Shockwave, the *rollover* command lets you do much more that. We'll look at some more creative examples of *rollover* in the following examples.

Winter Wonderland

Figure 3-3 shows the opening graphic of a Shockwave movie I created for a self-promotional holiday greeting. The opening graphic shows a winter village at night. Moving the mouse around the scene lights up the dark buildings; passing the mouse over lit buildings turns the lights off. This is all done with *rollover,* although the script is somewhat more involved than our first one.

The cast of this movie is shown in Figure 3-4. Cast member 1 is the background image of the dark town. Members 2 through 24 are the graphics for the individual lit buildings.

See it in action
Winter Wonderland is located on the CD in *source/winter.dir.*

Figure 3-3. The *Winter Wonderland* scene with lights off (top) and on (bottom).

Creating Rollover Effects

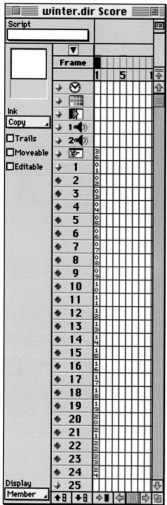

Figure 3-5. The *Winter Wonderland* score window.

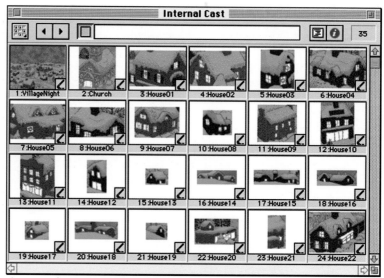

Figure 3-4. The *Winter Wonderland* cast window.

The movie uses 24 sprite channels, each channel containing one of the graphics from the cast. Sprite channel 1 contains the graphic in cast number 1, sprite channel 2 contains the graphic in cast member 2, and so on. The score is shown in Figure 3-5. At the start of the movie, the graphics in these channels have been made invisible, by turning their visibility off (note the depressed diamond shapes to the left of the channel numbers). The rollover process will make them visible one by one, turning the lights on.

In this movie everything happens inside a single frame. In the script channel, we have an *exitFrame* handler with a *go to the frame* command that keeps the movie looping on this frame. The trick here is to keep track of which buildings are lit and which are dark, and switch the lights on or off accordingly. Figure 3-6 shows the *enterFrame* handler that makes this work.

First the handler must identify whether the mouse is over any of the sprites. This is done with a *repeat* loop **A** that checks each sprite to see if it's visible or not. This part of the script creates a variable, *n,* and assigns a different sprite to that variable on each iteration of the loop. The loop starts with sprite 24 and goes down to sprite 2. The next step is to check whether the mouse is over sprite *n.* The command *rollover(n)* **B** checks whether the mouse is over the sprite.

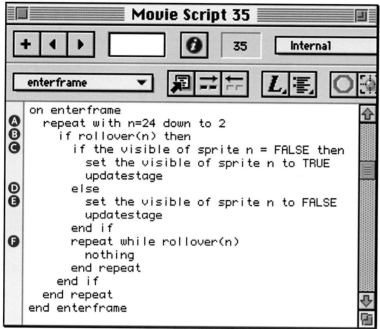

```
                  Movie Script 35

  +    ◀   ▶  [        ]   ⓘ    35       Internal

  enterframe        ▼   [icons]  L,≣,  ○ [icon]

Ⓐ  on enterframe
Ⓑ    repeat with n=24 down to 2
Ⓒ      if rollover(n) then
         if the visible of sprite n = FALSE then
           set the visible of sprite n to TRUE
           updatestage
Ⓓ        else
Ⓔ          set the visible of sprite n to FALSE
           updatestage
         end if
Ⓕ        repeat while rollover(n)
           nothing
         end repeat
       end if
     end repeat
   end enterframe
```

Figure 3-6. The *enterFrame* handler.

The script is based on a couple of *if ... then* statements. To understand how this works, it is helpful to take some specific examples. Let's say that *n* is sprite 24. The line *if rollover(n) then* says if the mouse is over sprite 24, execute the following code; if not, the repeat loop runs again, this time with *n* equal to 23. When the script identifies the sprite the mouse is over, it runs the code on the following lines.

At this point Ⓒ there is another *if ... then* statement. If the sprite is invisible (the visible equals false), then it is made visible (set the visible to true), and the stage is updated.

If the condition following *if* is not true, the code following *else* Ⓓ is run. That is, if the sprite is visible (the visible of the sprite is not false), the sprite is made invisible, Ⓔ and the stage is updated.

The next three lines Ⓕ simply run a repeat loop for as long as the mouse is over the sprite. This might seem like an unnecessary bit of code — after all, why should you have to specify that the script should do nothing; but in fact if you don't include this code, Shockwave continually swaps between the two

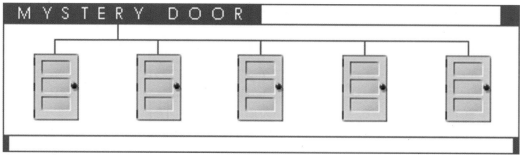

Figure 3-7. The opening stage for *Mystery Door*.

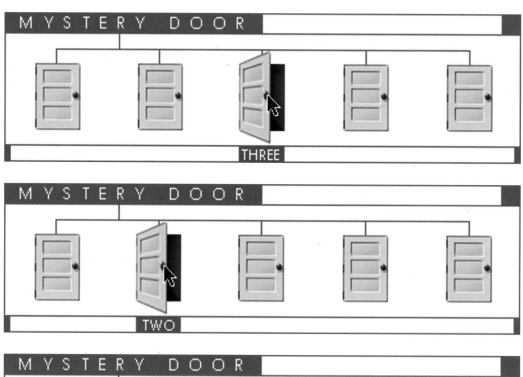

Figure 3-8. Rolling over a door opens it and displays the number beneath it.

states causing the lights to flash on and off rapidly. The rest of the script simply closes the remaining open statements. This simple structure is able to quickly check a variety of sprites for rollover using the same statements, rather than having to create individual *if...then* structures for each of the 23 sprite channels that contain the art of the individual buildings.

"Carol, what's behind door number three?!"

Let's look at another example that shows how creatively this technique can be used. The *Mystery Door* feature from my personal Web site uses a door metaphor to offer users a set of five mystery links. When the user moves the mouse over a door, it opens with a squeak and the number of the door appears below it. (See Figures 3-7 and 3-8.) When the mouse leaves, the door slams shut with a thump. Clicking on a door activates a link to a URL. This simple device adds interest, and an element of fun, to an otherwise static page of links.

If you look at the score for this example (Figure 3-9), you'll see it's set up with five separate placements of the closed-door cast member (number 2: Figure 3-10 shows the cast for this movie). These are in sprite channels 2, 4, 6, 8, and 10. Each door has a corresponding number graphic in the following sprite channel. For example, there's a closed door in sprite channel 2, and the "ONE" graphic (cast member 4) is in sprite channel 3. The subsequent

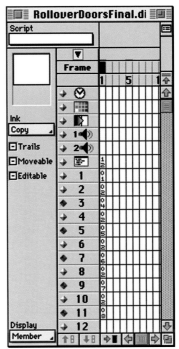

Figure 3-9. The score for *Mystery Door*.

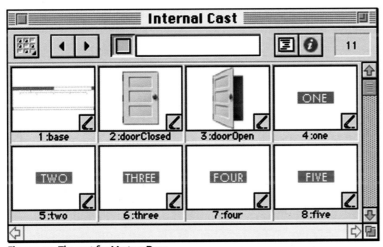

Figure 3-10. The cast for *Mystery Door*.

See it in action

Mystery Door is located on the CD in *source/door.dir*, and on the Web at *http://www.redrom. com/links/*

number graphics are in channels 5, 7, 9, and 11. All these number sprites are invisible at the start of the movie. We will make these channels visible with a rollover script.

First, let's look at the the *exitFrame* script contained in the script channel of frame 1 (Figure 3-11). After initializing a global variable (for more on variables and how to use them, see Chapter 4) called *gCurrentSprite*, Ⓐ the script immediately calls another script called *spriteCast*. Ⓑ This script (Figure 3-12) simply determines which door the mouse is over (if any) and puts that information into a global variable called *gCurrentSprite*. At this point let's switch over to *spriteCast*.

The *spriteCast* script

The first line of the *spriteCast* script initializes the global variable *gCurrentSprite*. Ⓐ Next the script executes a *case* statement. Ⓑ The *case* statement is a multibranching logic structure much like an *if...then* statement.

In this script, we are checking to see which door the mouse is over. (Remember, sprites 2, 4, 6, 8, and 10 contain doors) Rather than writing five *if...then* statements checking for *rollover(2), rollover(4),* etc., the *case* statement lets you quickly plug in a number of possible values into the function *rollover( )*. So the first line Ⓒ of the *case* statement checks for *rollover(2)*, which means the mouse is over the sprite in channel 2, and if it is, it sets the variable *gCurrentSprite* to the number 2. The *case* statement checks each line to see if the mouse is over any of the numbers indicated in the *case* statement and sets the variable *gCurrentSprite* to the appropriate number. It then exits the handler, returning to the *exitFrame* handler.

After the *spriteCast* handler has executed, the *exitFrame* script (Figure 3-11) starts an *if...then* statement. Ⓒ First it checks to see if the mouse is still over the same door as specified in *gCurrentSprite*. If so, it executes the remaining lines of code in the *if...then* structure.

For example, say the mouse is over the third door. The graphic for the third door is in channel 6, so *gCurrentSprite* equals 6. The next line Ⓓ puts the sprite in that channel under the control of Lingo. In the next line, Ⓔ the cast number of sprite 6 is changed to the number of the open-door graphic, named

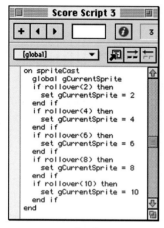

```
on spriteCast
   global gCurrentSprite
   if rollover(2) then
      set gCurrentSprite = 2
   end if
   if rollover(4) then
      set gCurrentSprite = 4
   end if
   if rollover(6) then
      set gCurrentSprite = 6
   end if
   if rollover(8) then
      set gCurrentSprite = 8
   end if
   if rollover(10) then
      set gCurrentSprite = 10
   end if
end
```

Case vs. *if...then*

The advantage of using the *case* statement instead of multiple *if...then* statements is that it is supposedly more efficient. Whether or not this is true is the subject of endless debate among Lingo experts. The use here is so short as to make the difference between *case* and *if...then* statements immaterial. One advantage *case* has over *if...then* statements is that it is easier and cleaner to code. For Shockwave users it offers the additional advantage of using fewer lines of code (compare the code in Figure 3-12 with the code above), which in the end saves on the byte size of the final movie. This is particularly important when you are trying to create very small, lean movies.

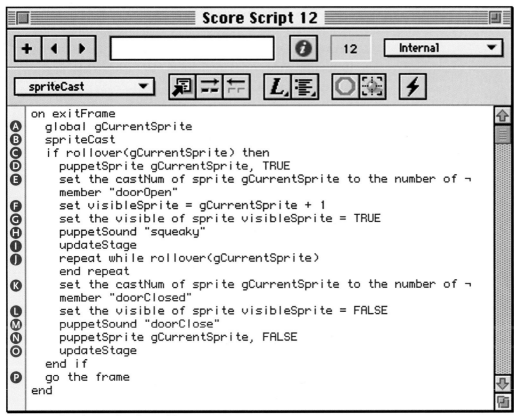

```
on exitFrame
  global gCurrentSprite
  spriteCast
  if rollover(gCurrentSprite) then
    puppetSprite gCurrentSprite, TRUE
    set the castNum of sprite gCurrentSprite to the number of ¬
      member "doorOpen"
    set visibleSprite = gCurrentSprite + 1
    set the visible of sprite visibleSprite = TRUE
    puppetSound "squeaky"
    updateStage
    repeat while rollover(gCurrentSprite)
    end repeat
    set the castNum of sprite gCurrentSprite to the number of ¬
      member "doorClosed"
    set the visible of sprite visibleSprite = FALSE
    puppetSound "doorClose"
    puppetSprite gCurrentSprite, FALSE
    updateStage
  end if
  go the frame
end
```

Figure 3-11. The *exitFrame* handler used in *Mystery Door.*

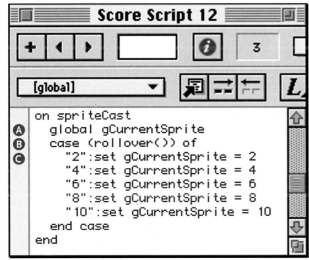

```
on spriteCast
  global gCurrentSprite
  case (rollover()) of
    "2":set gCurrentSprite = 2
    "4":set gCurrentSprite = 4
    "6":set gCurrentSprite = 6
    "8":set gCurrentSprite = 8
    "10":set gCurrentSprite = 10
  end case
end
```

Figure 3-12. The *spriteCast* handler.

doorOpen. This changes the closed door graphic to the opened door graphic. Next ❶ a local variable called *visibleSprite* adds 1 to the number of the current sprite (here, 6 + 1 = 7). In the next line ❻ the invisible sprite in channel 7 is turned visible. Remember, the graphic with the word "THREE" is in sprite channel 7.

After this, the script plays the sound called *squeaky,* ❽ which is the sound of a door creaking open. The stage is updated to show the graphic change. ❶ The script then repeats, doing nothing, while the mouse is still over the sprite in channel 6. ❶ This has the effect of pausing the movie until the user moves the mouse off the door graphic.

Once the mouse is moved off the third door, the cast number of the sprite in channel 6 is swapped with the number of the cast of the closed door *(doorClosed)*. ❷ The graphic of the word THREE in channel 7 *(visibleSprite)* is then turned invisible again ❶ and the sound of the door slamming *(doorClose)* is played. ❿ The sprite in channel 6 is taken out of Lingo's control ❶ and the stage is once again updated to show the change. ❶ That concludes the *if...then* statement and the final command ❶ is executed, sending the movie back to the beginning of frame 1, starting the process over again.

Although this script is a little more complex than creating separate *if...then* statements for each instance of the door on the stage, the movie will execute faster as the code is more efficient. In fact, this method uses five times fewer lines of code than a script with multiple *if...then* statements would.

By now you should have some idea of the many different ways in which rollovers can enhance your Web site and start seeing how commands are structured in Lingo to provide a variety of results. In the next chapter we'll look more closely at variables and what they can do to further enhance your projects.

4 The Power of Variables

In the last chapter, you got a taste of one of the simplest, yet most powerful, aspects of authoring with Shockwave — variables. Variables are essentially empty containers that hold information. Beyond this simple definition lies the foundation of just about every Director movie ever written. In fact, it may very well be impossible to create any but the simplest of interactions without using variables.

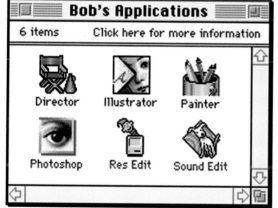

Figure 4-1. The interface for this movie is a Macintosh window with clickable icons.

Continuing with the theme of animating icons used in Chapter 2, this project will show a good example of how variables can be used for animation. We'll encounter variables in just about every example in this book, though, and their uses are as varied as the Director movies themselves.

In this project, clicking on different hot spots on each of the icons in the *Bob's Applications* window (Figure 4-1) launches different animations, 21 in all. Without variables, we'd have to write separate scripts for each animation. But in this project, we have just one animation script that utilizes a number of variables — and 21 little handler scripts that change the settings of those variables.

Each animation uses different cast members and plays different sounds; some need to loop, some don't, and others need an in-between loop. All of these attributes are controlled using variables.

Setting up the interactivity

Now let's take a look at how the moving icons project was created. The movie represents an open Macintosh window. After importing the base window art and placing it on the stage, followed by each of the individual program icons, we're ready to create clickable hot spots. Each icon will perform three different animations, so each needs three clickable areas (except for the Photoshop icon, which has seven clickable areas). The hot spots were created by making an unfilled rectangular shape with Director's *Tool* palette and placing it multiple times on the stage, one for each clickable area (as represented by the red shaded areas in Figure 4-2).

A *mouseUp* script is attached to each of these rectangles. Each script sets a different animation into motion when the user clicks

See it in action

To see the entire sequence play, open the movie *source/icons.dir* from the CD. Play the movie and click on the lower left-hand side of the Director icon. You will see that, although there is a lot happening in this movie, the entire sequence takes just a few seconds for Shockwave to execute.

Variable basics

Before looking at this project, we need to understand a few things about variables.

- **There are two kinds of variables: local and global.** A *local variable* is temporary; the value contained in the variable is retained only in the script that created it and is cleared when the script is over. The value contained in a *global variable,* on the other hand, is retained from script to script (and even from movie to movie) and is not cleared unless explicitly done so in Lingo.

- **Variables must first be initialized (given a name and assigned a value).** With a local variable, the variable is named and the value set at the same time. For example, the Lingo *set myVariable to 1* creates a local variable called *myVariable* and gives it a value of 1.

  With global variables, you must first declare the variable with the Lingo command *global.* To create a global variable called *myVariable,* you would first enter the line *global myVariable.* This variable will then be available throughout the movie. You can change its value with a line like *set myVariable to 1* or *put 1 into myVariable.*

- **Variables can be named anything you want.** A variable name can be as short as a single letter or long and complicated. It helps to choose names that indicate the variable's function; for example, *soundToPlayNext* would be a good name for a variable that contains the name of a sound to play.

on the spot. Figure 4-3 shows one of these *mouseUp* scripts.

Each *mouseUp* script, attached to the invisible rectangles, simply calls one of 21 custom handlers: *blink, tear, look, blue, green, red, yellow, paint, film, head, pencil, slate, flower, draw, pop, crack, winpop, evileye, tongue, wiggle, wag,* or *moof.* These handlers first set all the variables for the individual animations, then set that animation in motion by calling the *animateMe* script.

For a look at all the animations and their associated handler names, take a look at the following two pages.

To sum up, clicking on a hot spot runs a *mouseUp* script, which in turn calls a handler. The handler sets values for a number of variables and then runs the *animateMe* script, plugging those values into the script.

All the animations are separated into three parts or less. The first part is the basic animation. Some of the animations consist of just this first part. Some animations also include a *reverse loop,* in which the animation plays backwards; this is the last part. And some animations also include a sequence that bridges the first and last parts; this is the *in-between loop.*

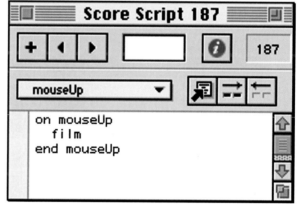

Figure 4-2. The red shaded areas indicate where the clickable hotspots in the movie are located.

Figure 4-3. This *mouseUp* script calls the *film* handler when the user clicks the lower-left portion of the Director icon.

Now let's look at the handler for the *film* animation, shown in Figure 4-4. This is the same animation we created in Chapter 2, so you should be familiar with how it works. It includes all three animation parts: the basic animation, the in-between loop, and the reverse loop.

The film handler has the simple task of setting values for the variables and then calling the *animateMe* script. Let's take a look at the names of the variables and what each of their functions are:

These next two pages show all of the animations in this project, and the handler names that go with them.

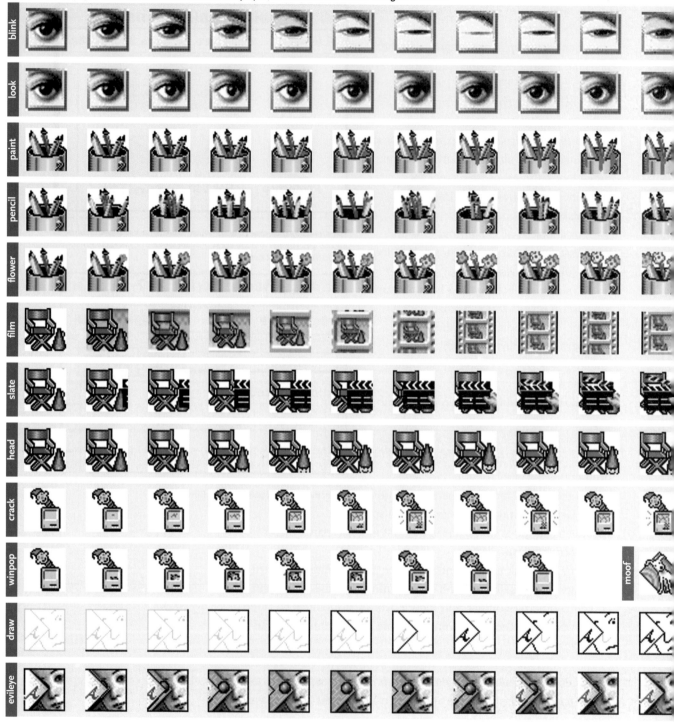

Note that the *green, yellow,* and *blue* handlers (not shown) function the same as the *red* handler.

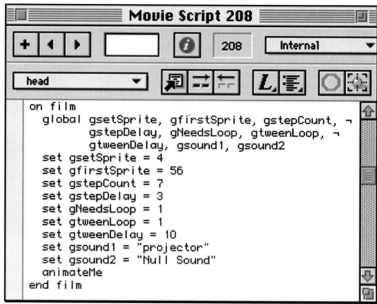

Figure 4-4. The *film* handler.

gsetSprite — The number of the score sprite channel where the animation will occur. In this case, it is set to 4, which is the channel that the Director icon is in.

gfirstSprite — Contains the cast number of the first sprite in the animation. Figure 4-5 shows the cast for this project. The value in this case is 56.

gstepCount — This relates to the number of cast members in the animation. I've called it *gstepCount* because, as you will see in the *animateMe* script, this number is used to step through the cast members of the animation. You'll notice in the cast window (Figure 4-5), that there are nine cast members (numbers 56-64) for this animation. So why is this variable set to 7? Because the first cast member is already on the stage and the last cast member is a part of the in-between loop (the rolling film sequence).

gstepDelay — This sets the frame rate of the animation by specifying the number of ticks to wait before the next frame is displayed. Here, this number has been set to 3. As there are 60 ticks per second, a three-tick delay means this animation will play at 20 frames per second (60 divided by 3).

Lingo tip

Often, Lingo authors will place a *g* in front of global variables to serve as a reminder that they are global variables as opposed to local variables.

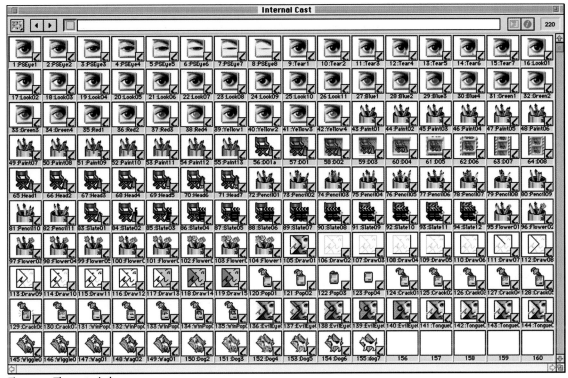

Figure 4-5. The cast window.

gneedsLoop — Indicates whether or not a *reverse loop* (the animation played backwards) will run after the animation plays. A value of 1 means there is a reverse loop; 0 means there is none. While most of the animations do use a reverse loop, for some it's undesirable to reverse the animation. For example, in the Photoshop eye, it would look awfully odd if, after the tear drop fell, the animation reversed and the tear drop went back up into the eye.

gtweenLoop — This variable does the same sort of thing as the *gneedsLoop* variable. Several of the animations, the *film* animation included, have a loop in between the first loop of the animation and the reverse loop at the end. Again a 1 indicates the presence of the in-between loop, and 0 means there is none.

gtweenDelay — Sets a delay between running the in-between loop and the last part of the animation. For the film animation, we need a slight delay at the point where the running filmstrip animation transitions back to the director's chair.

gsound1 — This is the sound that will play during the first part of the animation. In this animation it's the sound of a projector running.

gsound2 — The sound that will play during the reverse loop of the animation.

Once the *film* script has set all these variables, the last thing it does is call the *animateMe* script.

Animation time

The *animateMe* script is comprised of three main sections, as shown in Figure 4-6.

The first part of this script controls the beginning of the animation. For the film animation, that's the transition from the Director icon to the filmstrip. The next part controls the in-between loop of the animation, if needed. In this case, that's the running filmstrip portion of the animation. Finally, the last part of the script is the reverse loop of the animation, transitioning from the filmstrip back to the Director icon. Now let's break down this script line by line.

The first loop

After all the global variables have been declared, enabling them to be used in this handler, the script uses the *puppetSprite* command ❶ to put the sprite in channel 4 (remember *gsetSprite* = 4) under the control of Lingo. This is necessary for Lingo to be able to switch cast members in and out of channel 4.

The next two lines ❷ create two new local variables, *spriteNow* and *spriteCount,* setting them to equal *gfirstSprite,* in this case 56. Next, using the *puppetSound* command, ❸ the script plays the sound cast member contained in *gsound1.* In the film animation, this is the projector sound.

After this, the script enters into a repeat loop. This line ❹ says to keep repeating the loop as long as the *spriteCount* (56 at the start of the film animation) is less than the sum of the values of *spriteNow* and *gstepCount* — 63 in this case.

The next line ❺ of the repeat loop adds 1 to the number in *spriteCount* (making it 57). Next, ❻ the cast number of the sprite

The *repeat* loop
The basic mechanism of the *animateMe* script is the *repeat* loop. In each of the three sections of the script, loops are used to step through a series of images that make up the animation. The various aspects of the animations, such as the number of times the loop repeats and which set of graphics to use, are defined by the variables described earlier.

Lingo tip
You must declare the global variables to tell Lingo that it will be using their contents in this handler. If they're not declared, Lingo treats them as local variables, initializing them when they're called. Not declaring the global variables, means they would always be empty, causing a script error, as it is trying to use variables that have not yet been assigned values.

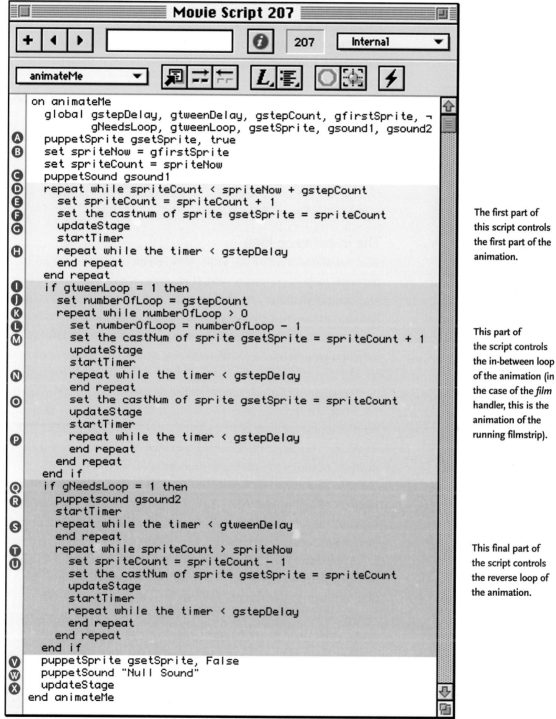

```
on animateMe
    global gstepDelay, gtweenDelay, gstepCount, gfirstSprite, ¬
          gNeedsLoop, gtweenLoop, gsetSprite, gsound1, gsound2
    puppetSprite gsetSprite, true
    set spriteNow = gfirstSprite
    set spriteCount = spriteNow
    puppetSound gsound1
    repeat while spriteCount < spriteNow + gstepCount
      set spriteCount = spriteCount + 1
      set the castnum of sprite gsetSprite = spriteCount
      updateStage
      startTimer
      repeat while the timer < gstepDelay
      end repeat
    end repeat
    if gtweenLoop = 1 then
      set numberOfLoop = gstepCount
      repeat while numberOfLoop > 0
        set numberOfLoop = numberOfLoop - 1
        set the castNum of sprite gsetSprite = spriteCount + 1
        updateStage
        startTimer
        repeat while the timer < gstepDelay
        end repeat
        set the castNum of sprite gsetSprite = spriteCount
        updateStage
        startTimer
        repeat while the timer < gstepDelay
        end repeat
      end repeat
    end if
    if gNeedsLoop = 1 then
      puppetsound gsound2
      startTimer
      repeat while the timer < gtweenDelay
      end repeat
      repeat while spriteCount > spriteNow
        set spriteCount = spriteCount - 1
        set the castNum of sprite gsetSprite = spriteCount
        updateStage
        startTimer
        repeat while the timer < gstepDelay
        end repeat
      end repeat
    end if
    puppetSprite gsetSprite, False
    puppetSound "Null Sound"
    updateStage
end animateMe
```

The first part of this script controls the first part of the animation.

This part of the script controls the in-between loop of the animation (in the case of the *film* handler, this is the animation of the running filmstrip).

This final part of the script controls the reverse loop of the animation.

Figure 4-6. The *animateMe* script.

in *gsetSprite* (channel 4) is made equal to the number in *spriteCount,* which was just changed from 56 to 57 in the previous line. These two lines give the mechanism of playing the animation: increase the value of the variable by 1, then use that value for the cast number of the sprite.

The final few commands in this first part of the script update the stage to show the change, **G** and set up a repeat loop **H** to delay the in-between steps of the animation as described earlier in the *gstepDelay* variable. The first repeat will loop until the value in *spriteCount* equals 64. It will then have stepped through cast members 56–63, and will exit the repeat loop and move on to the second part of the script.

The in-between loop

This middle section of the *animateMe* script determines if an in-between loop is necessary and, if so, executes it. The in-between loop simply displays two frames over and over again; in the film handler, these are cast members 63 and 64. This whole section is an *if...then* statement. The first line checks to see if the in-between loop is required. **I** In this case it is (since *gtweenLoop* is set to 1), so the rest of the statement is executed; if it were set to 0, this whole section would be skipped.

First, we create a new variable called *numberOfLoop* **J** and set it to equal the number in *gstepCount* (7, according to the *film* handler). This variable is simply a device to count down the number of times the loop will execute.

Next, we start another repeat loop **K** which loops as long as *numberOfLoop* equals more than 0. The next line **L** reduces the value of the variable by 1 each time through the loop. This creates our countdown effect.

The rest of this repeat loop sets the cast number of the sprite to increase by 1 (*spriteCount +1*); **M** in the film animation this sets the cast number to 64. After a three-tick delay loop, **N** similar to those described earlier, the sprite is then switched back to the value held in *spriteCount* (cast number 63). **O** There's another delay **P** and then the loop repeats. After the loop has repeated seven times (remember we're counting down from 7, the value of *gstepCount)*, this repeat loop ends and the script moves on to the third and last portion of the animation.

The reverse loop

The last part of the *animateMe* script reverses the first loop, if needed. As in the last section, a value of 1 for *gneedsLoop* means the loop exists; 0 means it doesn't. And once again there is an *if...then* statement, **Q** so if the variable equals 1, the commands in the statement are executed; if not, the script ends.

This section starts by playing the sound in the variable *gsound2*. **R** Next, a repeat loop starts, **S** which creates a delay before the loop is performed. This delay is required for aesthetic reasons; here it's 10 ticks — the value contained in *gtweenDelay*.

Now, another repeat loop **T** starts. This loop is similar to the script's first repeat loop, the only difference being that the number in *spriteCount* is reduced (not increased) by 1, **U** causing the film animation to play backwards. This loop continues for as long as the number in *spriteCount* is greater than the number in *spriteNow* (56). Once all the iterations of this final loop are completed, the repeat loop is exited and the final commands in the script are executed.

The *puppetSprite* command takes the sprite in channel 4 out of the control of Lingo. **V** Next, an empty sound called *Null Sound* is played. **W** This sound effectively stops any sound still playing, so sound won't continue beyond the end of the animation. Lastly, the stage is updated **X** as the *animateMe* script comes to an end.

This is just one example of how variables can be used in Director as powerful tools. In the next chapter, we'll explore an example of using variables in concert with lists to create dynamic game play.

5 Using Lists in Shockwave

In this chapter we'll discuss a game called *Cajones De Luminaire,* which is a digital version of the old Simon game many of us owned as kids. In Simon, as you'll recall, the idea was to repeat a sequence of lights and tones in the same order that the game played them. When you successfully complete one sequence, the game plays a longer sequence, which you must then repeat.

Cajones does much the same thing but adds a medium level in which the sequence plays faster with each round, and a hard level in which each sequence is completely different than the previous one. A game like this involves keeping track of lots of dynamic information; for instance, the sequence played by the game, the sequence played by the user, the length of the sequences, and so on.

To handle these demands, the authors of Cajones — an outfit called Funklab — used *lists,* a simple yet powerful aspect of Lingo. As the terms suggests, lists are simply containers for a series of items. You can use lists to hold important user data like names, addresses, high scores, or the answers to questions. In Cajones, one list stores a bunch of handlers, which are randomly accessed and stored in other lists for use by the game. This will all make more sense as we get into the Lingo that makes up Cajones.

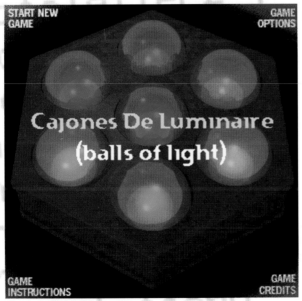

Figure 5-1. The opening screen to *Cajones De Luminaire.*

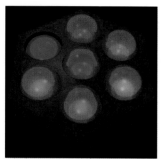 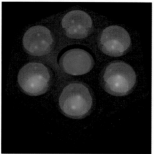 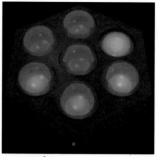 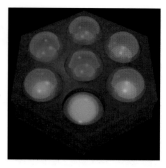

Figure 5-2. Cajones plays a sequence of flashing lights and sounds that the player must match.

Cajones offers three difficulty levels. On Easy, each successive sequence is one light longer than the previous sequence. The first sequence consists of one tone, the second two tones, and so on. As the user matches the sequences, Cajones generates longer and longer seqences, which the user must match. On Medium, game play is the same, but the sequences play faster and faster, eventually playing the tones in rapid

See it in action

Cajones De Luminaire is located on the CD in *source/cajones.dir.*

Also located on the disc is another movie created by Funklab called, *Hang That Man* (above). It's located at *source/ hangman.dir.*

Cajones' global variables

gmasterlist — There are 60 entries in this list; each entry is chosen at random from a list of seven choices, one for each colored light. This list is the master list for the order of lights and sound tones that the game will play. Sixty entries means Cajones can go up to only 60 levels on the easy and medium settings. This list is not used on the hard level.

gsimonlist — This is the progressive list that records the sequence that the game plays. On easy and medium, this list is culled from the master list. On hard, this list is randomly generated for each round. Play on the hard level is theoretically unlimited, as the game can always randomly generate another sequence.

guserlist — This list keeps track of the order in which the player clicks on balls during his turn.

gtonenums — This variable keeps track of the number of tones generated by the game in the current round. Unlike

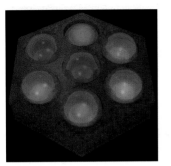 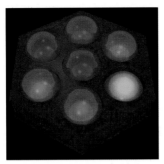 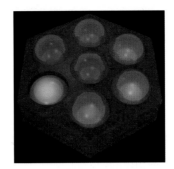 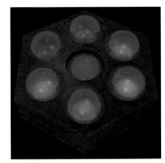

succession. On Hard, each sequence is a completely new pattern, making play much more difficult as the levels increase.

These sequences are all generated by creating a master play list by randomly selecting from seven handlers. From this list, the game plays the light and tone sequences. Another list keeps track of user play. At the easy and medium settings, new sequences are generated by appending a new handler to the

gsimonlist and *guserlist,* which contain actual handler names, *gtonenums* and *gusertone* only record the *number* of tones generated.

gusertone — Records the number of tones generated by the player during his turn.

guserstate — Keeps track of whose turn it is. There are three possible values: 0 means it's the game's turn, 1 means it's the player's turn, and 3 means the game is over.

gskill — Records the player's skill level: 1 indicates the easy level, 2 the medium level, and 3 the hard level. This variable is initially set to 1.

gbeeptime — This variable gives the time delay between tones. On the easy and hard levels, this delay stays constant at a half-second. On medium, the number is reduced by one-thirtieth of a second after each round, causing the game to play faster and faster with each round.

Funklab
http://www.funklab.com/

Josh Rosenfeld, President
Geoff Hoffman, Vice-president
Brian Bossin, Senior Designer
Jason Burke, Director of Technology
Andrew Shirk, Lingo Scripting

existing play list. On the hard level, a new sequence list is generated for every round. While that seems simple enough on the surface, the scripting actually gets rather complicated, as there are multiple skill levels to contend with and an array of variables necessary to keep track of game play. Let's go inside Cajones and see how it's put together.

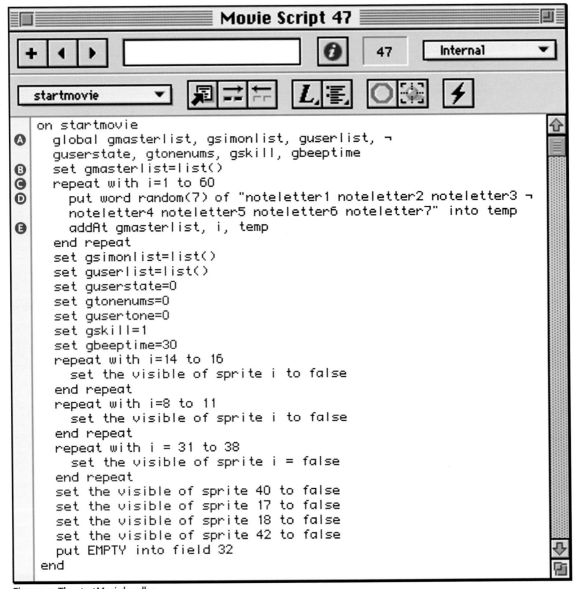

```
on startmovie
  global gmasterlist, gsimonlist, guserlist, ¬
  guserstate, gtonenums, gskill, gbeeptime
  set gmasterlist=list()
  repeat with i=1 to 60
    put word random(7) of "noteletter1 noteletter2 noteletter3 ¬
    noteletter4 noteletter5 noteletter6 noteletter7" into temp
    addAt gmasterlist, i, temp
  end repeat
  set gsimonlist=list()
  set guserlist=list()
  set guserstate=0
  set gtonenums=0
  set gusertone=0
  set gskill=1
  set gbeeptime=30
  repeat with i=14 to 16
    set the visible of sprite i to false
  end repeat
  repeat with i=8 to 11
    set the visible of sprite i to false
  end repeat
  repeat with i = 31 to 38
    set the visible of sprite i = false
  end repeat
  set the visible of sprite 40 to false
  set the visible of sprite 17 to false
  set the visible of sprite 18 to false
  set the visible of sprite 42 to false
  put EMPTY into field 32
end
```

Figure 5-3. The *startMovie* handler.

Shockwave Studio

The place to begin is the *startMovie* handler (Figure 5-3). First of all the script creates the custom lists and variables that the movie will use. 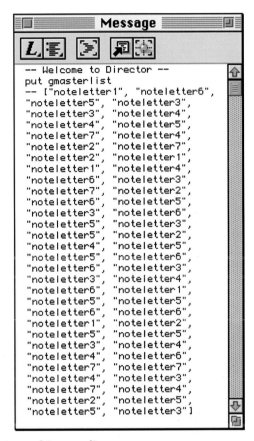 **A** The lists and variables used in Cajones are discussed in the sidebar, "Cajones' Global Variables."

Once the global lists and variables have been initialized, we need to create the master list of 60 randomly generated tones. First, *gmasterlist* is converted to an empty linear list by using the *list( )* function. **B** Next, a repeat loop executes 60 times **C** with the value of a local variable *i* increasing by 1 each time through the loop. On the first loop *i* = 1, on the second loop *i* = 2, and so on until *i* = 60. In this loop, the script places one of seven handler names, chosen at random, into another local variable named *temp*. **D**

The critical part of this statement is the *random( )* function, which picks at random a number between 1 and the number specified in the parentheses (in this case, 7). Following the command is a series of words; the *random* command will pick one of these words each time through the loop. For example, if the number 3 is chosen, the third word in this series is selected and put into the variable *temp*. In this example, *temp = noteletter3*.

At this point you may be asking yourself, what is *noteletter3*? To Lingo it means nothing — yet. Lingo thinks it's just a word and moves on to the next item in the script. What Lingo doesn't know at this point is that these *noteletter* expressions are the names of custom handlers that control the light and sound effects for each of the balls. We'll look at how these handlers work in the section, "The noteletterX handlers."

The final item in the repeat loop is the *addAt* command. **E** This line tells Lingo to add the

Peeking at lists

By using Director's *Message* window, you can take a look at the *gmasterlist* after the game has built it. Open the file *cajones.dir* in Director and start it playing. Select *Window/Message* and type the command *put gmasterlist* into the open *Message* window and hit *Return*. The window will then display the contents of *gmasterlist* as in the example seen above.

cajones.dir Score

Figure 5-4. The score window.

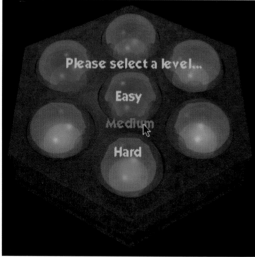

Figure 5-5. After the opening "splash" sequence plays, the game stops on this frame and waits for the user to select one of three difficulty settings.

contents of *temp* to the master list *(gmasterlist)* — at position number *i*. Since *i* increases by 1 with each iteration, the list grows one handler longer each time through the loop.

To give you an idea of how this works, let's go through an example sequence here. Let's say that the first loop gives a value of 1, the second loop gives a value 6, and the third loop gives a value of 5. The *addAt* command builds *gmasterlist* as follows:

1st loop	noteletter1
2nd loop	noteletter1, noteletter6
3rd loop	noteletter1, noteletter6, noteletter5

Although this repeat loop took a lot of words to explain, it takes the game only a fraction of a second to execute the code.

The rest of this *startMovie* handler is used to assign initial starting values to the lists and variables described earlier, and make invisible certain sprites. These sprites include the text for the game difficulty levels, the corner interface buttons, the lighted ball graphics (to be turned on by the *noteletterX* handlers), and text for the game credits, instructions, and final score.

Highlighting the skill settings

After Lingo finishes the *startMovie* handler, a splash screen sequence starts. An opening animation runs, there's a pause and then a random series of lights and tones plays; the movie then comes to a stop on frame 31 in the score (Figure 5-4), which contains the *exitFrame* handler seen in Figure 5-6.

The function of this handler is to check to see if the mouse is over the words "Easy," "Medium," or "Hard" and, if so, to change the color of that word to red (Figure 5-5). Once again, this is accomplished with the use of a repeat loop. Ⓐ

This loop is set to repeat three times with the local variable *i* given a value of 14, 15, or 16. These numbers correspond to the sprite channels that contain the three words. The first time through the loop, Lingo checks to see if the mouse is over the sprite in channel 14 (the word "Easy"). ❸ If it is, the color of sprite 14 is changed to red (the 35th color in the palette). ❹ If the mouse is not over that sprite (< > means "does not equal"), the forecolor is set to yellow (the 5th color in the palette). ❺ This loop is then repeated for the words "Medium" (sprite 15) and "Hard" (sprite 16).

At the end of the script is a *go to the frame* command, ❺ which causes the *exitFrame* handler to execute again, by sending the movie to the beginning of the same frame and repeating the rollover check. This repeats endlessly until the user clicks on one of the skill levels.

Choosing a player skill level

Attached to each of the skill level words ("Easy," "Medium," and "Hard") is one of three different *mouseUp* handlers that are executed when they are clicked on.

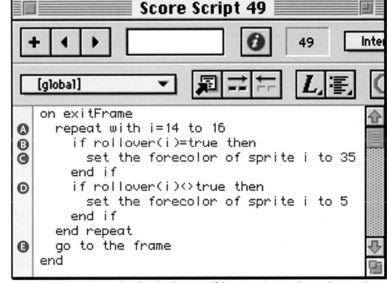

Figure 5-6. The *exitFrame* handler checks to see if the mouse is over the words "Easy," "Medium," or "Hard."

Let's take a look at the script attached to the word "Medium" (Figure 5-7):

First the script declares the global variable *gskill*. ❹ As you will recall, *gskill* was given an initial value of 1 in the *startMovie* handler. We have to declare this variable in this script so Lingo knows we will be working with it here.

Next the script calls the *startMovie* handler. ❸ This resets the game to its initial values, which may be important if the user was previously playing at another level.

To learn more about setting custom cursors see Chapter 6, *Doodlin' in Director.*

The two *puppetSprite* commands **C** transfer control of sprites 13 and 15 (the headline "Please select a level" and the word "Medium") from Lingo to the stage. This prevents sprites 13 and 15 carrying over to the next frame. The script then sends the movie to the next frame. **D** After this, a repeat loop sets the cursor for each of the ball sprites to an open hand, instead of the arrow cursor. **E**

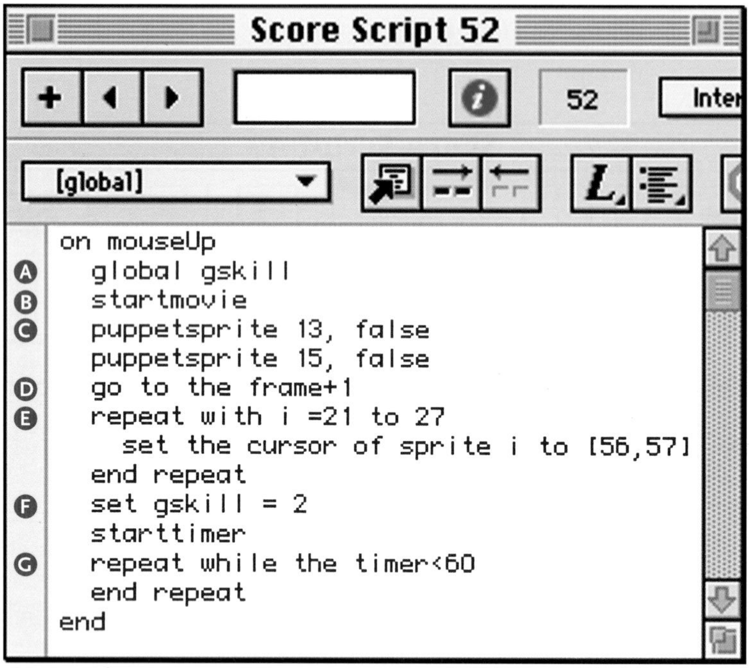

Next, and most importantly, the *gskill* variable is set to 2, **F** which corresponds to the medium skill level. You'll see why this is so important in the next section.

Finally, Lingo goes into another repeat loop **G** that delays the movie for 1 second (there are 60 ticks in a second). This gives Lingo time to finish all these functions before moving on.

```
Score Script 52                52        Inter

[global]

on mouseUp
A    global gskill
B    startmovie
C    puppetsprite 13, false
     puppetsprite 15, false
D    go to the frame+1
E    repeat with i =21 to 27
       set the cursor of sprite i to [56,57]
     end repeat
F    set gskill = 2
     starttimer
G    repeat while the timer<60
     end repeat
end
```

Figure 5-7. The *mouseUp* script attached to the word "Medium."

The corner buttons

Once the skill level has been chosen, the game enters the next frame, which contains an *exitFrame* handler (Figure 5-8). This handler executes as soon as the movie exits the frame. At the end of this *exitFrame* handler is a *go to the frame* command that causes the movie to loop back to the current frame, causing this *exitFrame* handler to be executed over and over again.

The first part of this handler calls *guserstate* **A** (the variable that contains the game status) and makes sure that the game is still on by checking the value of *guserstate*. **B** If it equals 3, the game is over and Lingo skips down to the *go to the frame* command.

If *guserstate* is not equal to 3, then the script proceeds with the *if...then* statement. This statement turns on each of the four corner interface elements ("Start New Game," "Game Options," "Game Instructions," and "Game Credits") if the mouse is over

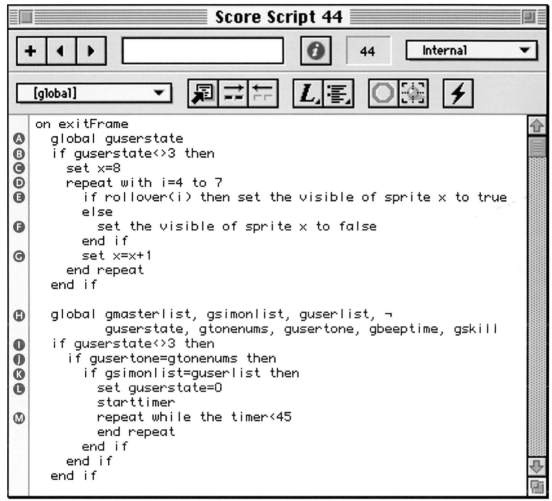

```
                    Score Script 44

  +   ◀  ▶  [                    ]   ⓘ   44    Internal  ▼

  [global]           ▼   🗗 ⇄ ← L ⫶ ◯ ⬚ 🗲

     on exitFrame
Ⓐ     global guserstate
Ⓑ     if guserstate<>3 then
Ⓒ       set x=8
Ⓓ       repeat with i=4 to 7
Ⓔ         if rollover(i) then set the visible of sprite x to true
           else
Ⓕ           set the visible of sprite x to false
           end if
Ⓖ         set x=x+1
         end repeat
       end if

Ⓗ     global gmasterlist, gsimonlist, guserlist, ¬
             guserstate, gtonenums, gusertone, gbeeptime, gskill
Ⓘ     if guserstate<>3 then
Ⓙ       if gusertone=gtonenums then
Ⓚ         if gsimonlist=guserlist then
Ⓛ           set guserstate=0
             starttimer
Ⓜ           repeat while the timer<45
             end repeat
           end if
         end if
       end if
```

Figure 5-8. The first part of the *exitFrame* that handler controls much of the game's play.

them (figure 5-9). The graphics for these corner elements are in
sprite channels 8–11, which were made invisible in the *startMovie*
handler. Also in each of the four corners are unfilled rectangle
shapes. These shapes are in sprite channels 4–7 and are used to
check if the mouse is in one of the corners.

   This is done by creating a local variable called *x*, which is
given a value of 8. Ⓒ This value corresponds to the "Start New
Game" graphic, located in sprite channel 8. Next a repeat loop is
executed four times with the variable *i* equal to 4 through 7. Ⓓ

These values relate to the sprite channels that hold the four unfilled corner shapes. The *rollover* command checks to see if the mouse is over the sprite indicated by *i*.  If it is over the sprite, the corresponding graphic is made visible. The first time through, Lingo is checking for the mouse over sprite 4 (the top-left corner); if it is over sprite 4, sprite 8 is made visible. If not, sprite 8 is made invisible. **F** The next line changes the value of *x* to 9 (*x = x + 1*). **G** The loop then makes sprite 9 visible if the mouse is over sprite 5. The process continues for the other two corners.

Figure 5-9. The four corner interface elements.

START NEW GAME

GAME OPTIONS

GAME INSTRUCTIONS

GAME CREDITS

After checking the corners, the game declares several of the global variables for use with this script **H** and makes sure the game is not over. **I**

Next, an *if...then* statement checks to see if the number of tones the user has clicked on (*gusertone*) equals the number of tones generated by the game for that round (*gtonenums*). **J** If they're not the same, then the player is still clicking balls and the script skips to the *go to the frame* statement. If the player has finished clicking balls, the script checks to see if *gsimonlist* (the list of tones played by the game) is the same as *guserlist* (the list of tones that the user played). **K** If it is, the user state is set to 0, **L** indicating that it is the game's turn to play tones. A repeat loop **M** then executes, causing a slight delay in the movie. After this, the game moves on to play the sequence of lights and tones for this round.

Flashing lights and playing tones

Now we come to fun part — actually making the lights flash and emit tones. This part of the script is shown in Figure 5-10.

At this point, the script checks to see if it's the game's turn to play. If the user state is set to 0 then it is. **A** Next it checks to see if the player's skill level is set to hard (*gskill = 3*). **B** If true, the statements in the *if...then* structure are executed. If the player's skill level is not set to hard, the script skips the *then* portion of

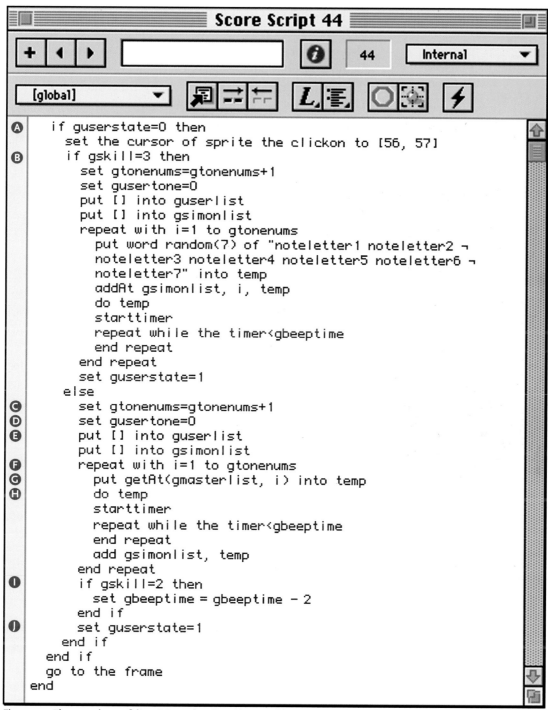

Figure 5-10. The second part of the *exitFrame* handler. This part of the script controls the flashing of the lights.

the script and goes right to the *else* portion. Let's put aside the hard level and look at the lines following the *else* statement. These statements control what happens on the easy and medium player skill level settings.

The first command **C** increases by 1 the value of *gtonenums*, the variable that tells the game how many lights and tones to play in this round. Thus each sequence is one tone longer than the previous one.

Next the script sets *gusertone* (the number of tones clicked on by the user) back to 0. **D** In the initial round this value will already be set to 0, but in subsequent rounds it needs to be reset. Just as important is setting the lists *guserlist* and *gsimonlist* back to empty, which is done in the next two lines of code. **E**

Next the script proceeds to play the number of tones required for this round. This is done with another repeat loop. **F** The number of loops is determined by the value of *gtonenums*. For example, in the third round *gtonenums* equals 3. So this statement would translate as *repeat with i = 1 to 3*.

The next two lines get a handler name from the master list of handler names *(gmasterlist)* and execute that handler. The *getAt* command gets a *noteletterX* handler from the master list. **G** (Remember, back in the *startMovie* script (Figure 5-3), *gmasterlist* was generated by randomly picking from a list of seven *noteletterX* handlers.) In the first loop of this repeat, the first word (*i* being equal to 1) from *gmasterlist* is put into a local variable named *temp*. The next line instructs Lingo to execute the handler contained in *temp*. The next time through the loop, Lingo gets the next (*i* = 2) word in the master list, and so on.

After each tone plays, a repeat loop delays the movie slightly before playing the next tone. This loop delays the movie by the number of ticks specifed in *gbeeptime*. This variable contains an initial value of 30 ticks, or a half second. Longer delays make it easier to repeat the sequence; shorter delays make it harder. On the medium skill level, the value of *gbeeptime* is reduced by 2 ticks each time through the loop. After the delay, the notehandler is added to *gsimonlist* (the record of the game's sequence).

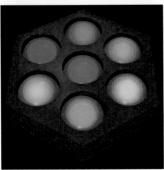

Figure 5-11. The Cajones game board consists of seven colored balls (top). Over each of these balls is placed a lit-up, depressed version (bottom). Each of these graphics have their visibility turned off at the start of the game. As game play progresses, these graphics are made visible, when needed, by the seven *noteletterX* handlers. This creates the illusion of the ball lighting up and being pressed in.

The *noteletterX* handlers

In the *startMovie* handler (Figure 5-3), *gmasterlist* was given 60 values chosen randomly from the words *noteletter1, noteletter2, noteletter3, noteletter4, noteletter5, noteletter6,* and *noteletter7*. Each of these words correspond to the name of a custom handler. These *noteletterX* handlers each light up one of the balls on the game board and play the tone associated with that ball (Figure 5-11). Let's take a look at how this is done by examining one of these handlers, *noteletter1*.

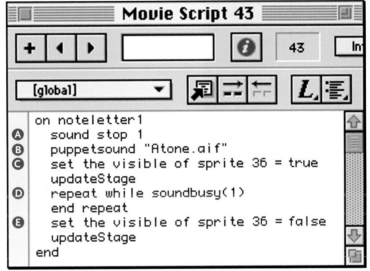

The first thing this handler (Figure 5-12) does is stop any sound playing in sound channel 1. **A** This prevents sounds carrying over from other *noteletterX* handlers stacking up on each other and throwing the flashing of the balls out of sync with their sounds. Next the *puppetSound* command plays the sound *Atone.aif.* **B** After this, the script makes sprite 36 (the

```
on noteletter1
    sound stop 1
    puppetsound "Atone.aif"
    set the visible of sprite 36 = true
    updateStage
    repeat while soundbusy(1)
    end repeat
    set the visible of sprite 36 = false
    updateStage
end
```

Figure 5-12. The *noteletter1* handler.

graphic of the blue ball, shown in Figure 5-13) visible **C** and updates the stage. This sprite is positioned over the unlit blue ball graphic and, when made visible, it looks as if the ball depresses and the blue light turns on.

The handler then enters into a repeat loop **D** that delays the movie until the *puppetSound* finishes playing in channel 1. It then completes the light flashing effect by turning off the visiblility of sprite 36. **E**

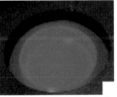

Figure 5-13. The lit blue ball graphic.

After finishing the *noteletterX* handler, the game returns to the repeat loop in the *exitFrame* handler at the point where it left (Figure 5-10, **H**). After executing all the iterations of the repeat loop, the script then checks to see if the skill level is set to Medium. **I** If it is, the delay between tones is reduced by 2 ticks. The *guserstate* variable is then set to 1, indicating it is the player's turn. **J**

The player's turn to click balls

Once the game has taken its turn and played its sequence of lights and sounds, it waits for user input. User input comes in the form of mouse clicks on any of the seven colored balls. Each of the colored balls on the game's board has an unfilled, unstroked oval shape over it, matching the shape of each ball. Each of these oval sprites has a sprite script attached. These sprite scripts contain *mouseDown* handlers that are activated when the sprite is clicked on. Each of these seven scripts (one for each colored ball) does essentially the same thing, except for a few variable changes like the color of the ball and the sound that it plays. Let's look at the *mouseDown* handler for the blue ball (Figure 5-15).

First the cursor is changed to the smaller hand. ❶ This adds to the effect of the ball being depressed when clicked on (Figure 5-14). After declaring the globals to be used in this script, the handler checks to see if the user state is 3 (game over). ❷ If the game is not over, the handler checks to see if the number of balls the player has clicked on *(gusertone)* is equal to the number of tones the game played in that round *(gtonenums)*. ❸ If the numbers are the same, it is the game's turn and the user state is set to 0. ❹ If the numbers are not the same, the handler goes on. In the next *if...then* statement ❺ the handler first checks to see if it is still the player's turn *(guserstate = 1)*.

If it is still the player's turn, the script adds 1 to *gusertone* (the number of balls the player has clicked) ❻ and then runs the *noteletter1* handler, ❼ which flashes the blue light and plays its sound. After finishing the *noteletter1* handler, the *mouseDown* script picks up where it left off. ❽ This statement adds the word "noteletter1" to *guserlist* (the list that keeps track of the balls the user has clicked on).

The next chunk of code checks to see if the user clicked on the correct ball. First, it puts into a variable called *temp* one of the words from the list *gsimonlist*, which word is determined by the value of *gusertone*. ❾ For example, if this is the third ball the player has clicked on, the value of *gusertone* would be 3, so the handler would put the third word of the list *gsimonlist* into *temp*.

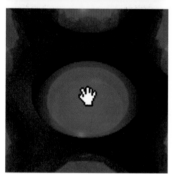

Figure 5-14. When the player clicks on a ball, the *mouseDown* script changes the standard hand cursor to a slightly smaller hand cursor. This adds to the illusion of the ball being depressed.

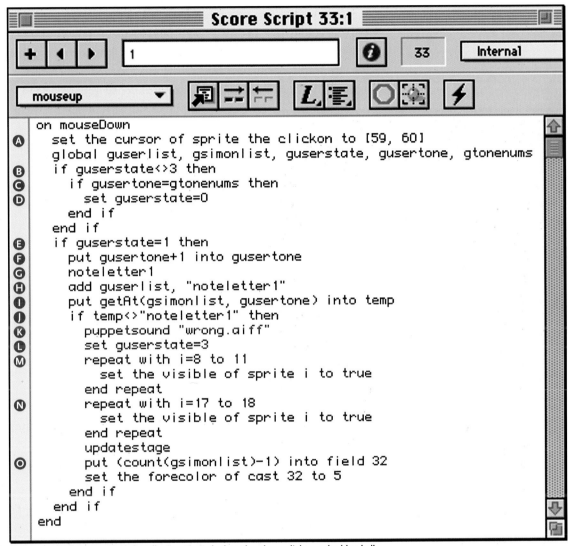

```
Score Script 33:1

+  ◀  ▶   [1                    ]    ℹ   33   Internal

mouseup        ▼   🔲🔲🔲  L🔲  ◯🔲  ⚡

  on mouseDown
A   set the cursor of sprite the clickon to [59, 60]
    global guserlist, gsimonlist, guserstate, gusertone, gtonenums
B   if guserstate<>3 then
C     if gusertone=gtonenums then
D       set guserstate=0
      end if
    end if
E   if guserstate=1 then
F     put gusertone+1 into gusertone
G     noteletter1
H     add guserlist, "noteletter1"
I     put getAt(gsimonlist, gusertone) into temp
J     if temp<>"noteletter1" then
K       puppetsound "wrong.aiff"
L       set guserstate=3
M       repeat with i=8 to 11
          set the visible of sprite i to true
        end repeat
N       repeat with i=17 to 18
          set the visible of sprite i to true
        end repeat
        updatestage
O       put (count(gsimonlist)-1) into field 32
        set the forecolor of cast 32 to 5
      end if
    end if
  end
```

Figure 5-15. This *mouseDown* handler is activated when the player clicks on the blue ball.

Next, the handler checks to see if the word in *temp* is *noteletter1*. **❶** If not, the player got it wrong and the game is over. If the word in *temp* is *noteletter1,* the player got it right and the handler is done. The game then waits for the next mouse click. If the player clicked on the wrong ball, the rest of the commands are executed.

First the sound *wrong.aiff* is played 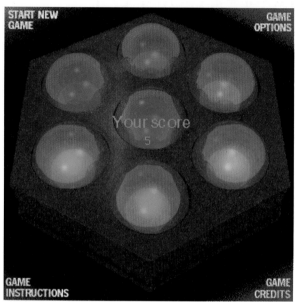 and the user state is set to 3 (game over). Next, two repeat loops take over. The first loop makes the interface elements in the four corners visible again, and the second makes the words "Your score" (sprite 17) and a text field below it (sprite 18) visible. This text field contains the player's final score, represented by the number of successfully completed levels (Figure 5-16). This number is calculated by subtracting 1 from the number of items in *gsimonlist* (to remove the current round that the player got wrong). That number is put into the text field in cast number 32, which is then colored green.

At this point the player has the option of selecting any of the four corner interface elements, or ending the game.

This concludes our look at one example of the power of using lists in Shockwave. By using lists we are able to compare values in one list with those in another, providing the ability to dynamically evaluate user input.

Now that we've looked at several of the available techniques (such as lists and variables) in Director to create dynamic content, the remainder of the book will concentrate on techniques for creating Shockwave movies that are "Net friendly." We'll talk about palettes, Net-specific Lingo commands, maximizing the user's experience, making movies smaller and, in the next chapter, techniques for enhancing your Shockwave movies.

Figure 5-16. The final screen of Cajones shows the number of successfully completed rounds.

6

Doodlin' in
Director

So far, we've used different techniques to produce variations on a simple animation sequence and learned a lot about the building blocks of Lingo — variables and lists. Starting with this chapter we'll discover a number of tips and techniques you can use to enhance your Shockwave projects and make them more Net-friendly.

The *Drag'n'Doodle* project I'll discuss in this chapter was originally part of a self-promotional CD-ROM project entitled *Toy Shelf.* The premise of the project was that multimedia isn't a new phenomena created by computers, CD-ROMS, or the Internet, but that many of our favorite childhood toys were actually "multimedia devices." *Toy Shelf* is split into three parts, each using one of my young daughter Hayley's toys as an interface element. The portfolio section used the venerable *Viewmaster,* calling it *ViewFolio* and combining text and pictures of my design samples. The *See 'n' Say* toy became an interactive interview session using QuickTime movies embedded in the toy interface. The last part of *Toy Shelf* is *Drag'n'Doodle* — which acted as the entry to my résumé section. Based on the popular

See it in action
Drag'n'Doodle is located on the CD in *source/ doodle.dir.* You can also see it on the Web at *http://www.redrom.com/ doodle/index.html.*

67

Creating the art

To illustrate the art for *Drag'n'Doodle,* I created the base shapes in Adobe Illustrator, drawing the shapes by eye, referencing my daughter's *MagnaDoodle.* After completing the basic line work, I pasted the Illustrator art into Adobe Photoshop, selecting *Paste As Paths* in the *Paste* dialog box (below). I then used these paths to create selections to illustrate the *Drag'n'Doodle* art (bottom). I illustrated certain items like the pen, the eraser handle, and the color hatch door on separate layers (right) to be able to create separate cast members from the one Photoshop file.

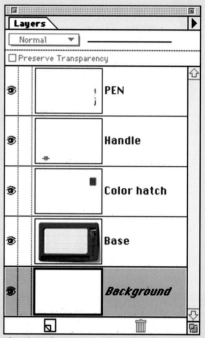

The Photoshop *Layers* palette showing each separate layer of the art.

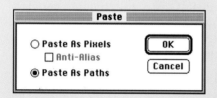

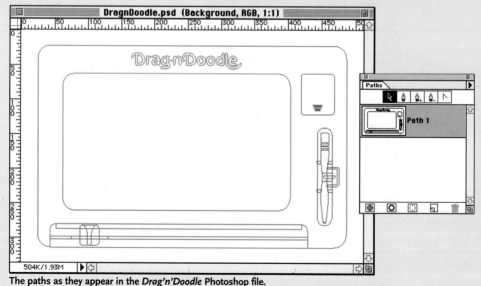

The paths as they appear in the *Drag'n'Doodle* Photoshop file.

MagnaDoodle drawing board, *Drag'n'Doodle* allowed users to sketch doodles as they read the text of my résumé.

Once Shockwave hit the Net, I was able to repurpose *Toy Shelf* into an online experience and distribute it much more widely — and cheaply. Of course with the Web there were a lot of new factors to consider, especially in terms of file size and bandwidth requirements. Drag'n'Doodle also presents many Director techniques that will be very useful in dressing up your own projects.

What we'll learn

- Drawing using sprite trails
- Drawing using *spriteBox*
- Changing colors on the fly
- Animating with built-in transitions
- Creating custom cursors
- Creating a slider

Draggin' and doodlin'

The *MagnaDoodle,* if you recall, had a magnetic pen and as you drew on the drawing surface, lines were formed by the magnet pulling metal filings to the underside of the board. You could clear your artwork by pulling the slider across the drawing board and wiping off the filings.

The *Drag'n'Doodle* works similarly, but we're pulling pixels instead of metal. That means we can draw in multiple colors instead of just black. Actually, in this process we're drawing with trails, not metal.

The basic method for drawing involves the use of Lingo's *trails of sprite* property. With this technique you create a sprite — in this case, a circle created with the Director's *Tool* palette — and set it to follow the mouse around the drawing area. The trail effect is turned on when the user holds the mouse button down over the drawing area and turned off when he lets go. The trail effect causes the sprite to leave a trail of copies of itself as it is moved around. Here's how it's done:

Figure 6-1. The Stage with the drawing sprite still visible in the lower-left corner. This dot, drawn with Director's ellipse tool, was nudged off-stage using the arrow keys.

To create the cast member used for the drawing sprite (sprite 4), I simply drew a small circle in the lower left-hand corner of the stage with Director's ellipse tool (Figure 6-1). I then used the arrow keys to nudge it off the bottom of the stage until it was no longer visible. This is so the user can't see the drawing sprite.

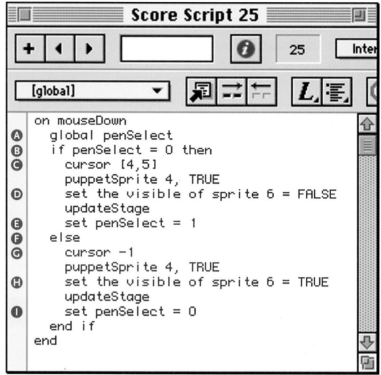

Figure 6-2. The *mouseDown* script is activated when the pen is clicked on.

The last cast member needed for this drawing technique is an invisible rectangular shape to act as the bounding area for the drawing surface. This shape (sprite number 5) was created with the rectangle tool. The rest is up to Lingo.

Selecting the pen

To start drawing, the user clicks on the pen in the lower right-hand corner. That click makes the pen disappear and changes the cursor from an arrow to a pencil. If the user has been drawing, clicking on the empty pen holder returns the pen to its place and changes the cursor back to an arrow. Both of these operations are accomplished with a *mouseDown* script (Figure 6-2) attached to an unfilled rectangle shape (located in sprite channel 19) positioned over the pen graphic .

The first line of this script declares the global variable *penSelect*. Ⓐ This variable indicates whether the user has picked up the pen or not. A value of 0 means the pen has not been clicked on; 1 means it has. This variable is initialized at the start of the movie, and given a value of 0. This *penSelect* variable is very important as it tells the *mouseDown* handler attached to the drawing area whether or not to let the user draw.

This script uses an *if...then* statement ❸ to control what to do based on whether the user has clicked on the pen or not. If not, the cursor is changed to a pencil icon. ❸ (Cast member number 4 is the pencil graphic and number 5 is the mask for the pencil. For more on setting custom cursors, see "Using Custom Mouse Cursors" later in this chapter.) The handler then turns the pen art (sprite 6) invisible, ❹ and sets *penSelect* to equal 1, ❸ indicating that the pen is active.

If the user has already selected the pen *(penSelect = 1)* this first portion of the script is ignored and the *else* portion ❻ is executed. These lines to do the opposite of the previous section. This part of the script changes the cursor from the pencil to the standard arrow (-1), ❺ makes the pen art visible again ❿ and sets the *penSelect* variable to equal 0. ❶

The pen graphic is a separate sprite positioned over the base *Drag'n'Doodle* graphic. This sprite is made invisible when clicked on.

The drawing action

When the user clicks within the drawing area (see Figure 6-3), another *mouseDown* script (Figure 6-4) is called, this one attached to sprite 5 (the bounding box of the drawing area).

After declaring the global variable *penSelect,* ❹ this script checks the status of the pen. If the pen is active *(penSelect = 1)*, the rest of the script is run. If not, the script ends. (Nothing happens if the user clicks in the drawing area while the pen is inactive.)

If the pen is active, a repeat loop starts. ❸ This loop continues the drawing action for as long as the mouse button is held down. Here's how it works: The vertical and horizontal positions of sprite 4 (the round dot) is set to match the vertical and horizontal positions of the mouse cursor. ❸

Next, the script checks to make sure the mouse hasn't moved off the drawing area (sprite 5). For this, another *if...then* statement

Figure 6-3. The red outline shows where sprite 5 (the bounding box of the drawing area) is positioned.

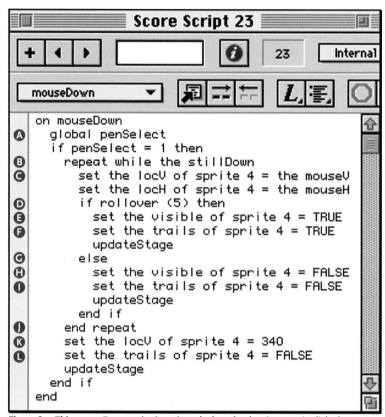

Figure 6-4. This *mouseDown* script is activated when the drawing area is clicked on.

is used. ❶ If the mouse is over sprite 5, then the script makes the round dot visible ❷ and turns on its trails property. ❸ If the mouse is not over the drawing area, ❹ the round dot is made invisible ❺ and the trails property turned off. ❻

When the mouse button is released, the repeat loop started with the line *repeat while the stillDown* ends. ❼ The vertical position of the round dot is then set to a position off the bottom of the stage ❽ and its trails property is turned off. ❾ This is done to avoid the last position of the round dot from disappearing, causing a break in the line that was just drawn. When the user begins drawing again, the *mouseDown* sequence restarts.

That's all there is to the basic drawing technique, but there is one drawback with this method: The stage can't always update

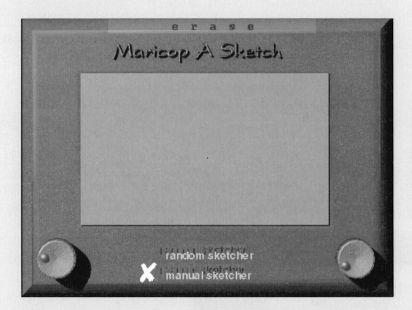

The Director Web
is located at *http://hakatai.
mcli.dist.maricopa.edu/
director/index.html* and has
many downloadable
samples of Director movies
including the *Maricop-A-
Sketch* by Alan Levine.

Maricop-A-Sketch and The Director Web

On the CD-ROM included with this book, you'll find the source
file of a sample illustrating one more drawing technique in
Director. It's called *sketch.dir* and it's located in the *source* folder.
This sample was created by Alan Levine, who maintains a site
called The Director Web.

This site, hosted by Maricopa Community Colleges in
Arizona, is one of the oldest established Director resources on the
Web — and by far the best. The Director Web gives directions on
joining Direct-L, the very popular and busy Listserv email
discussion list covering all aspects of Director authoring —
practical hands-on information from thousands of people actively
using Director. The Director Web also includes a wealth of news,
demos, FAQs, shareware, tips, scripts, XObjects, and resources for
the Director and Shockwave developer. If you have a question
about Director, Lingo, or Shockwave you'll most likely find the
answer here. Includes a searchable database. An indispensible
resource for Shockwave developers and it's all free!

itself fast enough, so if you're moving the mouse too quickly across the drawing area, you see a broken line of dots, rather than a solid line (as shown in Figure 6-5). If you'd prefer to avoid this behavior, you'll be interested in the *spriteBox* method, described in the next section.

See it in action
The version of *Drag'n'Doodle* using the *spriteBox* technique is located on the CD in *source/doodle2.dir.*

Drawing with *spriteBox*

The setup for this technique is almost identical to the previous technique. The main difference is that where we previously used a largish round dot — necessary to help minimize the skipping trails effect in the last technique — we're able to use a much smaller sprite, in this case a 1-pixel line created with Director's line tool.

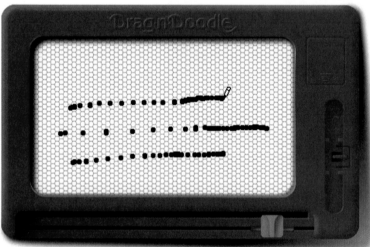

Figure 6-5. One drawback to the trails method of drawing in Director is that if the mouse is moved too quickly for the stage to update, the result will be a broken line.

The other difference in this technique is the Lingo used to create the drawing effect. First, let's look at the *mouseDown* script attached to sprite 5, (the bounding box for the drawing area), shown in Figure 6-6.

As in the previous technique, this script uses an *if...then* statement to determine whether the pen has been selected. If so, the script creates two custom variables, *oldV* and *oldH,* Ⓐ setting them to equal the current vertical and horizontal positions of the mouse cursor.

Next, the script enters into a repeat loop that repeats as long as the mouse button is held down. Ⓑ In this loop, an *if..then* statement checks to see if the mouse is still over the drawing area. Ⓒ If so, the script creates two more local variables, *newV* and *newH,* and sets them to equal the current vertical and horizontal positions of the mouse cursor. Ⓓ Next the script calls a custom handler called *drawLine* (which we'll explore shortly) and passes the handler four values, *oldV, oldH, newV,* and *newH.* Ⓔ

The *drawLine* handler will use these values to draw a line from the old vertical and horizontal positions to the new positions. If the mouse has moved, the numbers in the old and new variables will be different, and a line will be drawn. If the mouse hasn't moved, no line will be drawn.

The *drawLine* script

The first two lines of the *drawLine* handler script (Figure 6-7) use *if...then* statements to assure that the line is one pixel wide. **Ⓐ** This is done by comparing the old vertical and horizontal positions to the new ones. If they are the same, 1 is added to the old position. This rectifies a strange bit of behavior on Director's part. If the mouse moves in one direction only, there is no height to the sprite, so Director doesn't draw a line. Adding 1 pixel to the location creates the height necessary to draw the line.

After patching up this problem, the script uses *if...then* statements to determine the direction in which the cursor moved. It does this by comparing first the old and new vertical locations **Ⓑ Ⓔ** and then the horizontal locations. **Ⓒ Ⓓ Ⓕ Ⓖ** Once the direction of the cursor's travel has been determined, the bounding rectangle of sprite 4 (the 1-pixel line created earlier) is set using the *spriteBox* command.

```
Score Script 23

+  ◀  ▶    [      ]   ⓘ   23    Internal

mouseDown  ▼    ▣ ⇥ ⇤   L ☰

on mouseDown
   global penSelect
   if penSelect = 1 then
Ⓐ     set oldV = the mouseV
      set oldH = the mouseH
Ⓑ     repeat while the mouseDown
Ⓒ        if rollover(5) then
Ⓓ           set newV = the mouseV
            set newH = the mouseH
Ⓔ           drawLine(oldV, oldH, newV, newH)
Ⓕ           set oldV = newV
            set oldH = newH
         end if
      end repeat
   end if
end
```

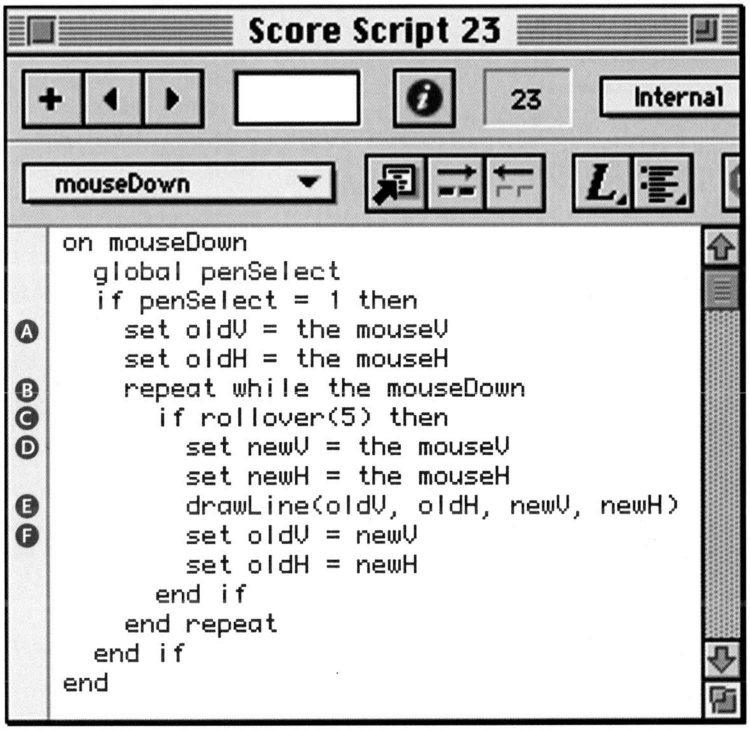

Figure 6-6. The *mouseDown* script for the *spriteBox* method.

Take section **Ⓒ** for example. This section is run if the new position is to the upper-left of the old position (that is, if the old vertical is greater than the new vertical and the old horizontal is greater than the new horizontal.) If this is the case, a bounding box for sprite 4 is drawn (that's the *spriteBox* command) with the left, top, right, and bottom coordinates (in that order) defined by the four values following the *spriteBox* command. Here the left

This *drawLine* script was
contributed by Lingo
author Matthew Caldwell.
His email address is:
sexkittn@burn.demon.co.uk.

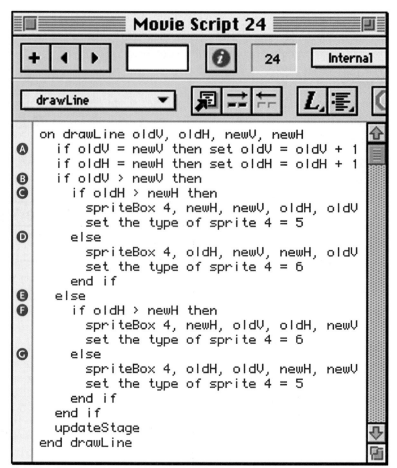

```
on drawLine oldV, oldH, newV, newH
   if oldV = newV then set oldV = oldV + 1
   if oldH = newH then set oldH = oldH + 1
   if oldV > newV then
     if oldH > newH then
       spriteBox 4, newH, newV, oldH, oldV
       set the type of sprite 4 = 5
     else
       spriteBox 4, oldH, newV, newH, oldV
       set the type of sprite 4 = 6
     end if
   else
     if oldH > newH then
       spriteBox 4, newH, oldV, oldH, newV
       set the type of sprite 4 = 6
     else
       spriteBox 4, oldH, oldV, newH, newV
       set the type of sprite 4 = 5
     end if
   end if
   updateStage
end drawLine
```

Figure 6-7. The *drawLine* script.

coordinate is the value of *newH*, the top is the value of *newV*, the
right is the value of *oldH*, and the bottom is the value of *oldV*.
You can see how the order of the coordinates changes in the
other sections.

The line following the *spriteBox* command sets sprite 4's *type*
to the appropriate state for the direction of the line. *Type of sprite
5* is a line drawn — within the bounding rectangle — from the
top left to bottom right, and *type of sprite 6* (used in sections **D**
and **E**) is a line drawn from the bottom left to the top right.

After updating the stage, this handler returns to the
mouseDown script, which picks up where it left off when the

Figure 6-8. The clickable areas of the color palette were created by placing nine unfilled rectangles on the stage, one over each of the color squares. Each of these rectangles has a *mouseUp* script attached to it, which changes the color of the drawing sprite.

drawLine handler was called. As you'll recall, the *mouseDown* handler (Figure 6-6) is in a repeat loop for as long as the mouse button is down. After the *drawLine* handler executes and returns the values, *oldV* and *oldH* are set to equal the values held in *newV* and *newH*. ❻ This whole process repeats itself for as long as the mouse button is held down.

While moving the mouse too quickly with this technique won't cause a broken line as in the previous technique — because the *drawLine* script is essentially drawing a straight line from one point to another — the lines tend to have more square edges and straightness, causing them to look less natural. As with the *trails of sprite* technique, the slower the user draws, the smoother the line.

Both techniques have their pros and cons; you'll have to choose which method best serves your purposes.

Changing colors with *forecolor*

One of the *Drag'n'Doodle's* main advantages over the *MagnaDoodle* is the ability to draw with a wider range of colors than just black. To accomplish this I used Lingo's *forecolor of sprite* property.

I created the clickable areas over the *Drag'n'Doodle's* color palette by making an unfilled, unstroked shape created with

Figure 6-9. One of the nine scripts for setting the color of the drawing shape (sprite 4).

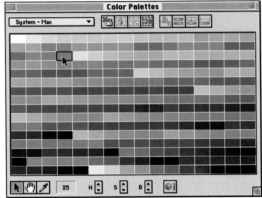

Figure 6-10. The *Color Palettes* window.

Director's rectangle tool. I created one cast member rectangle and reused it nine times on the stage — once for each color. After placing the nine sprites on the stage and positioning them over each of the color squares (Figure 6-8), I attached a simple script to each. An example of this is shown in Figure 6-9. In this example, we are simply setting the color (*forecolor*) of our drawing dot (sprite 4) to a bright red, the 35th color in the current palette. An easy way to determine the color numbers for use with the *forecolor* property is to consult the color palette window in Director. To access the palette, select **Window/Color Palettes.** This brings up the window shown in Figure 6-10. Simply choose the color you want to use by clicking on it in the palette and the corresponding number is displayed in a box at the bottom of the window.

Animating using transitions

One of the difficulties in designing multimedia for the Web is in keeping file sizes as small as possible so they download quickly. Anything you can do to minimize file size is to your benefit. One simple way to create a small animation is by using Director's built-in transitions. I used one such transition in order to animate the opening and closing of the color palette door. I could have spent a lot of precious byte space creating a traditional timeline-based animation of the door panel, making multiple versions of the panel getting shorter and shorter and then stepping them across multiple frames in a timeline animation. (We discussed this technique in Chapter 2). Instead I chose the more economical method of using a transition.

The first thing to do is create a beginning and ending state for the transition. The two states for this animation (the closed door and the

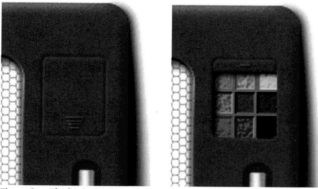

Figure 6-11. The beginning state (left) and ending state (right) for the color palette door. They are placed in frames 1 and 2 respectively.

open door) are shown in Figure 6-11. Next, we place the two states in the score in separate frames. A simple *go frame* script (Figure 6-12) is then attached to the closed door sprite; when the closed door is clicked on, the script sends the movie to the frame with the open door sprite in it.

On the frame with the open door in it, I placed a transition in the score's transition channel. To apply a transition to the transition panel, double-click in the transition channel for the frame you want the transition in. This brings up the *Transition* dialog box (Figure 6-13). This lets you choose the transition you

Figure 6-12. This script sends the movie to the frame labeled *color* when the color palette door is clicked.

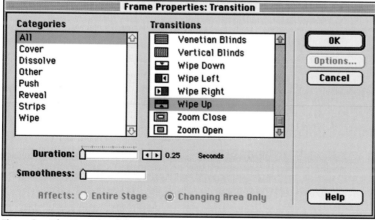

Figure 6-13. The *Transition* dialog box.

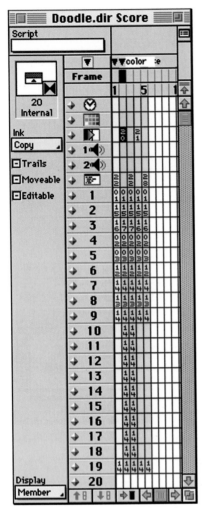

Figure 6-14. A look at the score shows the the setup for the transitions. Frame 1 (highlighted with yellow) contains the closed door sprite in channel 3 (cast member 16). The closed door sprite (cast member 17) is in frame 2 (highlighted with blue). The transition channel of frame 2 (highlighted with black) contains the *Wipe Up* transition. Frame 3 is a duplicate of frame 2 without the transition and the addition of a *go to the frame* script in the script channel. Channels 4 and 5 (highlighted in pink) use the *Wipe Down* transition to animate the door closing.

want, set the duration of the transition and the smoothness of the transition.

For *Drag'n'Doodle* I wanted to create the illusion of the door opening upward so I selected *Wipe Up*. I wanted the door to open quickly so as not to hinder the user's experience, but slowly enough so they would see the door opening. I found ¼ of a second to work ideally. I also wanted the door to slide up as smoothly as possible, so I set the *Smoothness* slider all the way to the left.

One last thing to keep in mind when using transitions in this way is not to use a *go to frame* loop on the frame with the transition. This will cause the transition to repeat itself over and over again in the frame. Although this won't be visible to the user, it will slow down the speed of the movie to a crawl. And, in the case of a project like *Drag'n'Doodle*, not only does it slow down the response, it refreshes the stage, causing the drawing trails to disappear as quickly as they are drawn.

The idea is to duplicate the transition frame over to the next frame and put the *go to the frame* statement in the *exitframe* handler to loop the movie there (Figure 6-14). This way the movie will hit the frame with the transition, do the transition once and move to the next frame, where the movie then loops.

Creating custom mouse cursors

Another easy method for spicing up movies without using up a lot of bytes is to use custom cursors. Director comes with several built-in cursors that can be accessed simply by calling them by their appropriate number (Figure 6-15). Examples of these are the arrow (-1), the text insertion I-beam (1), the crosshair (2), the plus symbol (3), the watch/hour glass (4), and a blank cursor (200) which allows you to hide the cursor from the user. Using 0 sets the cursor back to the system default, most likely the arrow.

Of course, these few choices don't offer much variety; in order to give the user more cursor feedback you need to create your own custom cursors. In *Drag'n'Doodle* I've used several custom cursors, a finger pointing, an open hand, a pencil, and a closed hand.

Custom cursors can be any 1-bit (black and white) cast member that is 16 x 16 pixels. Anything larger than 16 x 16 pixels is cropped from the upper left-hand corner. When you import a cursor graphic into Director make sure it's 1-bit by selecting it in the cast window and choosing **Cast/Transform Bitmap.** This brings up the *Transform Bitmap* dialog box (Figure 6-16). Transform the bitmap by selecting 1-bit from the *Color Depth* popup menu and clicking *OK.*

One trick for getting your cursors to work correctly is to create them 17 x 17 instead of 16 x 16. Add a one-pixel line of black to the bottom and right sides (Figure 6-17) These lines will be cropped off when the cursor is implemented in Lingo, but they create a bounding area for the cursor. This is particularly helpful if your cursor art isn't precisely 16 x 16 pixels, as is the case with the pencil cursor.

Another part of creating custom cursors is creating a cursor mask. The cursor mask is the area of the cursor that you want to be opaque white. If you don't create a mask for the cursor all the white areas of the cursor become transparent and only the black

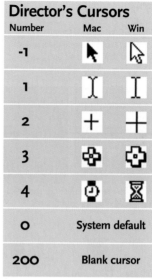

Director's Cursors

Number	Mac	Win
-1	↖	↖
1	I	I
2	+	+
3	✛	✛
4	⌚	⌛
0	System default	
200	Blank cursor	

Figure 6-15. Director's built-in cursors.

Transform Bitmap

Cast Member: Cast Member 4:Pencil

┌ Size: ─────
◉ Scale: `100` %
○ Width: `17` pixels
Height: `17` pixels

┌ Colors: ─────
Color Depth: `1 Bit`
Palette: `System — Mac`
◉ Dither
○ Remap to Closest Colors

[OK]
[Cancel]
[Help]

Figure 6-16. The *Transform Bitmap* dialog box.

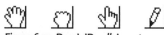
Figure 6-17. *Drag'n'Doodle's* custom cursors. Note the one-pixel line of black to the right and bottom.

Figure 6-18. The finger cursor with (left) and without (right) a mask.

Figure 6-19. The custom cursors with their accompanying masks.

lines show up. This can make a cursor very difficult to see against a busy or dark background (see Figure 6-18).

The mask art for a cursor is usually just a duplicate of the cursor filled with black where you want the white to appear (see Figure 6-19). If you want a white border around your cursor simply add a 1-pixel border around the mask art.

Again, the rest is up to Lingo. In *Drag'n'Doodle* I used the *cursor of sprite* property to assign different cursors to different sprites in the movie (Figure 6-20). First I start by setting the overall cursor to the System default. ❶ Next, I set the cursor of sprite properties for each of my stage elements. For sprite 3, the door hatch for the color tray, I set the cursor to cast number 10 (the finger) and the mask to cast number 11. ❷ The cast window, seen in Figure 6-21, shows the cast numbers of the cursors and their masks.

This is how all the the cursors are set. The first number in brackets represents the number of the cast member to be used for the cursor, and the second number represents the cast

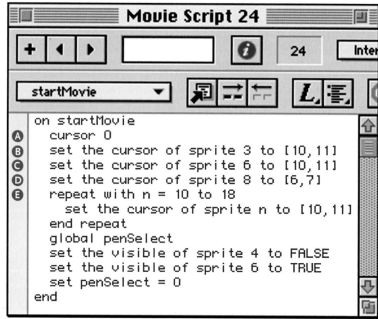

Figure 6-20. The cursors for each of the different sprites in the movie are set in the *startMovie* handler.

Shockwave Studio

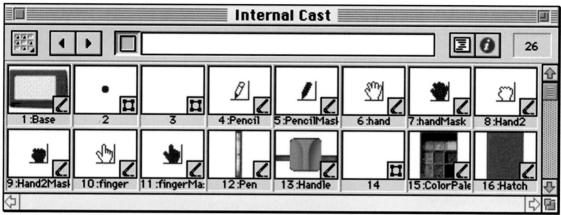

Figure 6-21. The cast window shows the cast numbers for each of the custom cursors and their masks.

member to be used as the cursor mask. For sprite 6 (the pen) I've set the cursor to the finger cursor, **C** for sprite 8 (the handle) I've set the cursor to the hand cursor, **D** and so on.

The repeat loop **E** represents a small trick to shave bytes from the file and save some wear and tear on your fingers by reducing the amount of typing you have to do. I have a series of sprites in a row that all need to have their cursor property set to the same cast numbers. Rather than creating nine separate lines of code to set each cursor individually, I've done the same thing in three lines of code using a repeat loop. Using a local variable called n, the Lingo repeats nine times with n equal to 10 the first time, 11 on the next loop, and so on through 18. Each time through, sprite number n is set to the finger cursor. Admittedly, this only saves about 6 lines of code, but in the small bandwidth world of the Web every byte counts.

Creating the slider

To create the eraser effect for *Drag'n'Doodle,* I used a combination of three sprites, one visible — the slider handle — and two invisible — the actual eraser and a constraining shape for the handle. When the user grabs the red handle and moves it across the drawing area, the invisible sprite — a rectangle about ½" wide that is as tall as the drawing area — follows, matching the horizontal position of the handle. Running this invisible

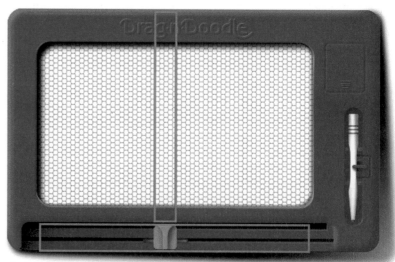

Figure 6-22. This figure shows the placement of the invisible sprites (outlined in red). One shape is placed over the drawing area. This shape erases the drawing as it is dragged back and forth by following the movement of the red handle. The second shape is placed over the slider area to constrain the handle's movement. By constraining to this graphic, the handle is prevented from moving too far to the left or right.

Ink effects

The red handle sprite is a separate graphic placed on the stage with the matte ink effect set. This makes the base art of the *Drag'n'Doodle* show through the white background of the handle art. See Chapter 7, *Making Smaller Movies,* for more on ink effects.

rectangle over the drawing area "erases" the trails effect of the pen tool. The trick here is to keep the handle constrained to the slider area of the illustration, so the user can't drag the slider all over the screen. To accomplish this, I've placed an invisible shape over the slider area (Figure 6-22), which I will use to prevent the handle from leaving the slider area. Let's look at the Lingo that constrains the handle and makes the eraser sprite follow its movement (Figure 6-23).

As soon as the user clicks on the slider handle, the script changes the cursor to a closed hand. ❶ Then sprites 8 and 9 are put under Lingo's control. ❷ The *moveableSprite* property is turned on for these sprites, ❸ so the user can move them with the mouse. Next comes a loop that repeats for as long as the mouse is down. ❹ Within this loop is where the mouse tracking and constraining takes place.

In the first line of the loop, ❺ the horizontal position of the handle (sprite 8) is set to the horizontal position of the mouse, yet it is constrained within the shape of sprite 7 (the unfilled, unstroked rectangle positioned to match the shape of the slider area).

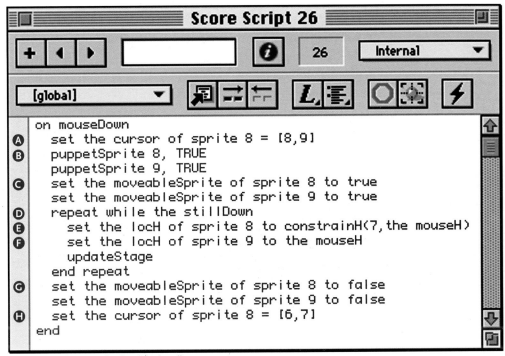

```
on mouseDown
    set the cursor of sprite 8 = [8,9]
    puppetSprite 8, TRUE
    puppetSprite 9, TRUE
    set the moveableSprite of sprite 8 to true
    set the moveableSprite of sprite 9 to true
    repeat while the stillDown
        set the locH of sprite 8 to constrainH(7,the mouseH)
        set the locH of sprite 9 to the mouseH
        updateStage
    end repeat
    set the moveableSprite of sprite 8 to false
    set the moveableSprite of sprite 9 to false
    set the cursor of sprite 8 = [6,7]
end
```

Figure 6-23. The script for the slider handle.

The Lingo command for this is *constrainH.* Inside the
parentheses are, first, the number of the sprite that the horizontal
location is constrained to, and, second, the value the horizontal
position should be set to given the constraining factor. In this
case it is the horizontal position of the mouse *(the mouseH).* The
effect is that as long as the horizontal position of the mouse *(the
mouseH)* is within the constraining box of sprite 7, the handle will
move to match the position of the mouse. Once the mouse
moves out of the constraining area, the handle stops moving.

In the next line **F** the horizontal position of sprite 9 (the
invisible ½" wide graphic in the drawing area) is set to the
horizontal position of the mouse. Finally, the stage is updated
and the repeat loop ends.

Once the mouse button is released by the user, Lingo exits
the repeat loop, turning off the movability of sprites 8 and 9 **G**
and changing the cursor of the handle back to the open hand. **H**

See it in action
The pumpkin carving game is located on the CD in *source/carver.dir*.

As a special Halloween treat for *Web Review* readers, I created a Shockwave pumpkin carving game (Figure 6-24). This game uses a variation on the doodling-with-trails effect described in this chapter.

Rather than drawing with trails, at the start of the movie a trailed image of the face of the pumpkin is left behind over the graphic of the interior of the pumpkin. Then a small graphic, following the cursor around, is used to erase the trailed face of the pumpkin. Let's take a look at how this effect is accomplished.

The base graphic consists of a night sky and the interior of a pumpkin sitting in a field of darkened grass (Figure 6-25). On top of this, I've placed a second graphic, the face of the pumpkin (Figure 6-26). In this technique, the front of the pumpkin is positioned over the background graphic and quickly moved out of the visible area of the movie with the trails ink on. Doing this leaves a single image of the pumpkin skin behind in the graphic's original position.

Figure 6-24. Carving the face of the pumpkin reveals the base graphic.

The nature of the trailed image — it's just a temporary copy of the graphic that it came from — allows us to create an eraser effect by bringing another invisible graphic across the pumpkin, following the mouse cursor. Rather than adding to the drawing, as we do in *Drag'n'Doodle*, we're carving away portions of the pumpkin skin revealing the inner pumpkin beneath it. Both of these things — the setting of the trails effect and the movement of the invisible graphic — are accomplished with Lingo.

Let's look at the Lingo that sets up the trail of the pumpkin face (Figure 6-27).

The first two lines of this *startMovie* handler 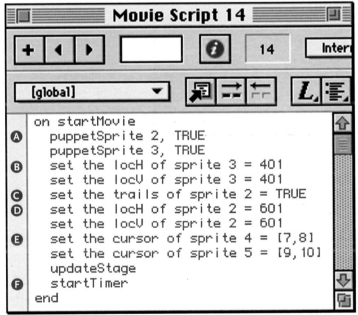Ⓐ use the *puppetSprite* command to put the sprites in channels 2 (the skin of the pumpkin) and 3 (the little, invisible eraser graphic) under the control of Lingo. The next two lines Ⓑ move the eraser graphic off the visible area of the stage, so the eraser won't leave behind any artifacts on the trailed image of the pumpkin when it is first moved to the cursor position. Next, the trails property of sprite 2 is turned on. Ⓒ The pumpkin skin graphic is then moved off the stage by setting its horizontal and vertical positions to a point outside the confines of the stage. Ⓓ The next two lines Ⓔ set up custom cursors for the face of the pumpkin and the little pumpkin button in the right-hand corner. After this, the stage is updated and the timer is started for use later in the movie. Ⓕ

With this handler, we've moved the skin of the pumpkin graphic off the stage, leaving in its place a trail of the image, which can now be manipulated by the user. This entire operation is instantaneous and completely invisible to the user.

Figure 6-25. The base graphic.

Figure 6-26. The face of the pumpkin.

```
═══ Movie Script 14 ═══

  +  ◀  ▶  [      ]  ⓘ  14  Inter

  [global]  ▼  📲 ➡ ⟵  L ≣

     on startMovie
Ⓐ      puppetSprite 2, TRUE
        puppetSprite 3, TRUE
Ⓑ      set the locH of sprite 3 = 401
        set the locV of sprite 3 = 401
Ⓒ      set the trails of sprite 2 = TRUE
Ⓓ      set the locH of sprite 2 = 601
        set the locV of sprite 2 = 601
Ⓔ      set the cursor of sprite 4 = [7,8]
        set the cursor of sprite 5 = [9,10]
        updateStage
Ⓕ      startTimer
     end
```

Figure 6-27. The *startMovie* script.

Virtual carving

Next let's look at what makes the carving possible. An unfilled, unstroked shape, created with Director's ellipse tool, has been placed over the entire face of the pumpkin. This shape is in sprite channel 4, and its only purpose is to capture the user's mouse clicks on the face of the pumpkin. When the user clicks on this invisible sprite, the *mouseDown* handler, shown in Figure 6-28, goes into effect.

First, sprite 3 (the eraser graphic) is placed in the control of Lingo with the *puppetSprite* command. **A** Next, the horizontal and vertical positions of the eraser are set to match the location of the mouse cursor minus 3 pixels. **B** We're subtracting 3 pixels from the mouse position to compensate for the registration point of the dot, which is set to the upper left-hand corner of the graphic. Because the dot is a shape cast (created with Director's *Tool* Palette), its registration point cannot be altered — unlike a bitmap graphic, which can

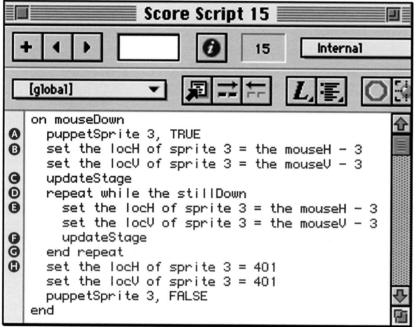

Figure 6-28. The *mouseDown* script creates the carving effect.

have its registration point repositioned. Without the offset, the registration point of the shape would map to the tip of the cursor and appear as if the eraser was beneath the cursor rather than directly on its tip. Offsetting the graphic positions it in the correct position. The next line **C** then updates the stage.

Following this, the handler enters into a repeat loop. **D** This loop repeats itself as long as the mouse button is held down. The loop continually moves sprite 3 (the eraser) to the location of the

 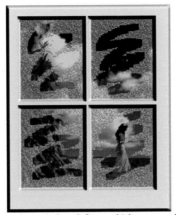 

Figure 6-29. *Sophia's Window* depicts a steamed up window (left) on which you can draw (center), revealing the scene outside the window (right). Another excellent example of this technique.

mouse **E** regardless of where the user may move it, and constantly updates the stage, **F** causing the eraser effect.

Once the mouse button is released, the repeat loop ends **G** and the final lines of code are executed. **H** The eraser graphic is moved off the stage again, and the last line of code takes it out of the control of Lingo, ending the carving function.

Gazing through *Sophia's Window*

Robert Lewis, an illustrator and designer based in Maryland, was so inspired after seeing my pumpkin carving technique in *Web Review,* that he quickly came up with his own clever application. *Sophia's Window* depicts a steamed up window (Figure 6-29) that the user can draw on, revealing a beautiful scene of a woman (presumably Sophia) walking in a harvest-time field. This is an excellent example of taking the techniques detailed here and applying them creatively to your own projects.

See it in action
Sophia's Window is located on the CD in *source/window.dir.*

7

Making Smaller Movies

When designing multimedia for the Web, the foremost consideration has to be file size. With most of the world connecting to the Net with 28.8K or slower modems, the size of your final file will determine whether the user sticks around to see your creation, or reaches quickly for the back button. Of course, users will be more willing to wait for a good game or interesting interface than for a huge file of a 3D company logo spinning on the page.

Regardless of the content of your movie, keeping the file size as small as possible is to everyone's advantage. In this chapter, we'll look at several examples that demonstrate interesting techniques that will help you take a "byte" out of the file sizes of your movies.

What we'll learn

Techniques for minimizing file size that we'll discuss in this chapter:

- Tiling backgrounds
- Ink effects
- Blending techniques
- Using 1-bit graphics

Tiling backgrounds

Director offers the ability to create custom repeating tiles from small cast member graphics, which can be used to cover large areas with no additional memory increase. This is accomplished by using the custom tile to fill shapes made with Director's *Tool* palette.

Mark Hager makes nice use of this technique in his *Times Square Marquee*, a Shockwave movie that creates a scrolling banner of lights, just like the Times Square marquee in New York City. TSM uses the Net-specific Lingo *getNetText* to read a text file from the Internet and display the text in lights on the Shockwave banner

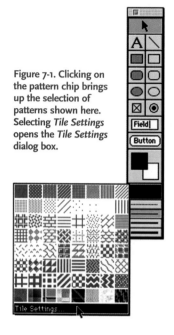

Figure 7-1. Clicking on the pattern chip brings up the selection of patterns shown here. Selecting *Tile Settings* opens the *Tile Settings* dialog box.

(for more on Net-specific Lingo, see Chapter 9, *Using Net-Specific Lingo*). Changing the message is as simple as editing the text file and saving it to the server; Shockwave does the rest.

Let's look at how Mark used the tile technique to create his background of lights using a very small graphic.

To create a tile pattern in Director you first import the art you want to use into the cast of your movie. Mark created a tile, 16 x 16 pixels, of a repeating pattern of lights. Once the graphic for the tile is in the cast, it is an easy matter to make the tile itself.

First, click on the *pattern chip* in the *Tool* palette. This brings up the selection of patterns shown in Figure 7-1. Select *Tile Settings* at the bottom of this window to bring up the dialog box shown in Figure 7-2.

Director comes with eight predefined tile patterns, which are shown next to the word *Edit*. Below that are two boxes that show the current selected tile. The box on the left shows the tile itself and allows you to select which portion of the graphic to use in the pattern. The box on the right shows a preview of what the pattern will look like.

To make your tile, select the *Cast Member* radio button from the *Source* area. This activates the arrow buttons to the right.

Tile sizes

Director's tile sizes are predefined and can range from 16 pixels to 128 pixels in 16, 32, 64, or 128 pixel increments. The tile does not have to be square, but its height and width must be one of these four dimensions. For example, you could have tiles measuring 16x64, 128x32 or 64x32, etc.

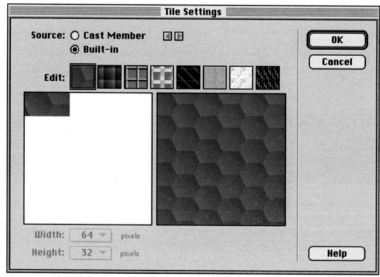

Figure 7-2. The *Tile Settings* dialog box.

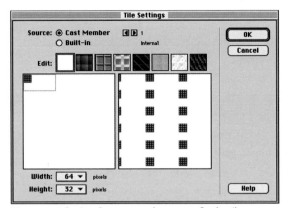

Figure 7-3. Selecting the cast member source for the tile.

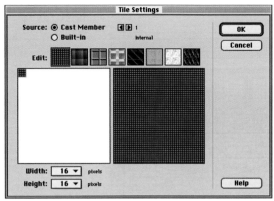

Figure 7-4. The tile with the correct width and height.

These allow you to click through the available cast members and select the one to use for the tile.

Figure 7-3 shows Mark's lights tile in the *Tile Settings* window. Note that the tile still has the size of the blue honeycomb tile it replaced. In the left-hand box, you can see the dashed line that defines the area of the tile. The 64 x 32-pixel bounding box of the previous pattern is too big for this tile, which causes the large areas of white in the right-hand preview box. We'll fix this by selecting 16 for both the width and height settings in the bottom-left corner (Figure 7-4).

Now the tile can be used within a rectangle shape to cover the stage in lights. Select the *Filled Rectangle* tool from the *Tool* palette (Figure 7-5) and use it to draw a rectangle covering the stage. The rectangle can then be filled with the newly created tile (Figure 7-6).

The 16 x 16 graphic used to create the tile is a meager 256 bytes (one-fourth of a kilobyte). By way of comparison, a graphic that fills the entire stage area would be a whopping 34K, or 136 times larger!

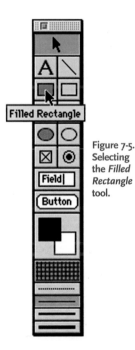

Figure 7-5. Selecting the *Filled Rectangle* tool.

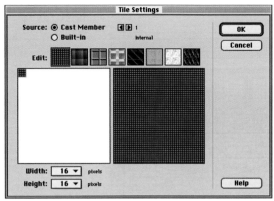

Figure 7-6. A rectangle shape, filled with the newly created tile, covers the stage in lights.

Ink effects

You can achieve many different effects with a single graphic by using Director's ink effects. These effects let you alter how graphics appear on the stage by changing how they interact with graphics on other layers. The effects are applied to graphics in the score window by selecting the graphic in its sprite channel and choosing one of the effects from the *Ink* popup menu (Figure 7-7).

Times Square Marquee makes use of ink effects very nicely. TSM uses over 200 separate graphics to illustrate every possible letter, number, and special character (see Figure 7-10). If each of these characters were illustrated in full color with lights in each, the final file size of the movie would be astronomical by Net standards. Mark instead uses very small gray and white graphics and the *Darkest* Ink effect to achieve the same results in a very small file size for each character. Figure 7-8 shows the words "Times Square Marquee" as they would normally appear on the stage with no ink effect set. In Figure 7-9 the *Darkest* ink effect has been applied to the graphic for each letter. Applying *Darkest* ink to the letter graphics causes only the colors that are darker than those in the graphic below to show. Lighter colors, like the white in the letters, are eliminated and the colored lights pattern shows through.

This is an excellent example of how custom tiles combined with ink effects can save a lot in the final file size of a movie, while still providing a dynamic graphic effect. Now, let's look at some other techniques to add to your bag of tricks for making smaller movies.

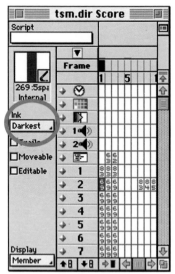

Figure 7-7. Ink effects are applied to sprites through the *Ink* popup menu (circled in red) in the score window.

See it in action

Times Square Marquee can be seen in action at Mark Hager's Mediæval Multimedia Web site at *http://www.mediaeval.nl/ lichtbak.html*. You can also find it on the CD at *source/tsm.dir*.

Figure 7-8. The graphics as they normally would appear on the Stage with their ink set to *Copy*.

Figure 7-9. The same graphics with the *Darkest* ink effect applied.

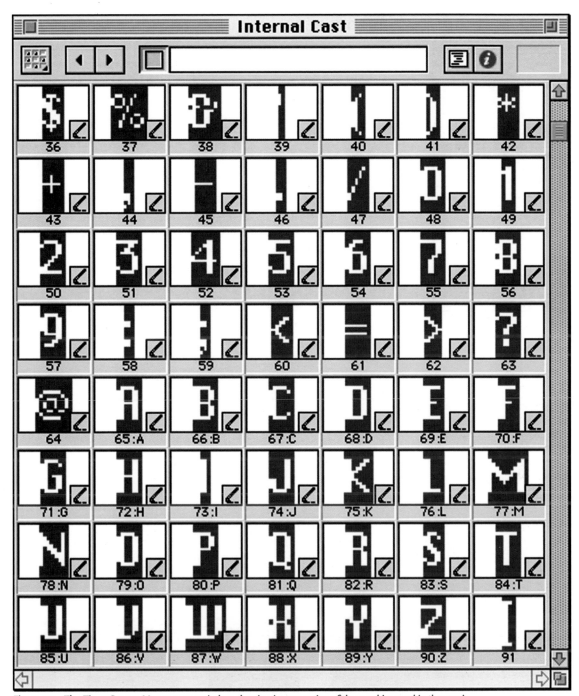

Figure 7-10. The *Times Square Marquee* cast window showing just a portion of the graphics used in the movie.

Blending techniques

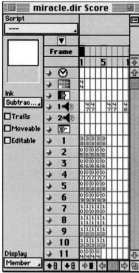

Figure 7-11. The score window.

In the opening banner headline for his site *The 40K Miracle* (see sidebar on page 98), Gabriel Jensen combines a *sprite blending* technique with custom tiles and ink effects to create a very realistic spotlight effect.

Gabriel built up the spotlight by layering 10 different graphics in the score (Figure 7-11). Let's look at how the effect was created.

The first layer of the spotlight effect is an oval filled with a custom tile created from the brick graphic seen in Figure 7-12. In the score, this graphic appears in sprite channel 1. Over this are nine layers (sprite channels 2 through 10) of concentric light yellow circle graphics (Figure 7-13). In Figure 7-14 we've made these graphics black so it is easier to see the nuances of each ring. All of these yellow graphics have their ink effects set to *Background Transparent,* which makes the white background of the graphics transparent. Also, each of these yellow graphics

Figure 7-12.

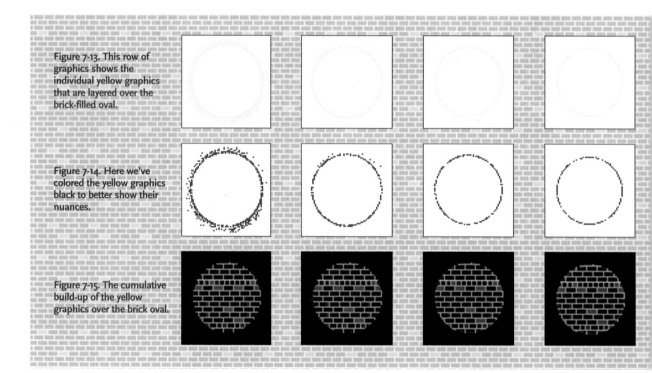

Figure 7-13. This row of graphics shows the individual yellow graphics that are layered over the brick-filled oval.

Figure 7-14. Here we've colored the yellow graphics black to better show their nuances.

Figure 7-15. The cumulative build-up of the yellow graphics over the brick oval.

have their *sprite blend property* set to a different percentage. The sprite blend property lets you control the opacity of a sprite. It is set in the *Sprite Properties* dialog box by entering a percentage into the *Blend* box (Figure 7-16).

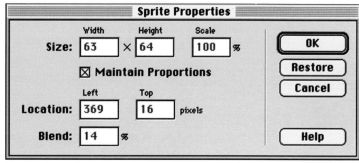

Each of the nine yellow graphics have their blend property set to incremental degrees of opacity, creating a soft, glowing effect around the edges of the spotlight area. Figure 7-15 shows this gradual build up of each layer of the yellow graphics. The effect is very subtle, yet provides a realistic sense of warmth to the lights.

Figure 7-16. The *Sprite Properties* dialog box.

Figure 7-17 shows a composite of all the layers of the circle graphics filled with different percentages of black, which demonstrates the cumulative effect of these graphics.

Figure 7-17.
The cumulative effect of all the blended graphics.

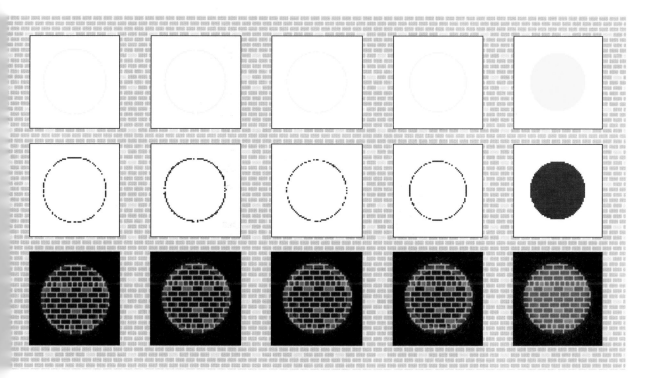

Another use for film loops

As the movie progresses, more and more spotlights turn on until the whole scene is awash in lights. By the end of the movie, there are 10 spotlights on the stage at the same time. At this point, you may be wondering, if there are only 48 sprite channels and each spotlight takes 10 channels each, how can there be that many lights on the stage simultaneously?

See it in action

The 40K Miracle can be seen on the Web at *http://www.40kmiracle.com/.* You can also find it on the CD at *source/miracle.dir.*

98   Shockwave Studio

This illustrates an excellent example of film loops in action. By capturing the information for the 10 sprites that make up the spotlight into a single film loop, Gabriel was able to place the film loop on the stage multiple times, using only one sprite channel instead of 10. In the end, the 10 lights on the stage take up only 10 sprite channels. (For more on film loops see Chapter 2, *Animating with Shockwave.*)

Gabriel Jensen. Gabriel also does custom Shockwave and Web site development through his company, Jig Software. They can be reached by email at *hello@jigsoftware.com*.

As the lights swing quickly back to the spot where the man was, we find he is gone.

With multiple popping sounds more spotlights begin to turn on.

Eight more spotlights turn on illuminating the words "The 40K Miracle."

Another spotlight reveals the man being carried back up to the ledge by two birds.

After the birds drop the man off and fly away, the dark sky brightens to light blue.

The 40K Miracle is an excellent example of how graphics with very small byte sizes can be combined with Director's ink effects, blends, and tiling to achieve some very creative results. Now let's look at one more technique that can help keep your movies small.

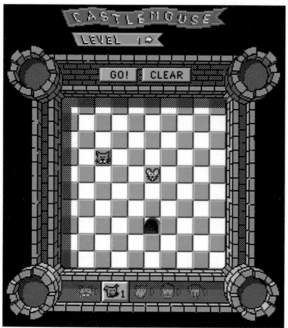

Figure 7-18. The first level of *Castle Mouse*.

Using 1-bit graphics

At the first mention of 1-bit graphics, most designers cringe. How can anything nice ever be done with 1-bit graphics? We've all seen those horrible Shockwave samples of photographic images turned into 1-bit graphics and paraded around the stage over the top of large areas of solid color. Hardly a satisfying effect.

I admit, the use of 1-bit graphics is limited at best, but — as we'll see in the next sample — with some careful thought and planning, a series of 1-bit graphics can be used very creatively — and go a long way toward reducing the file size of your movies.

Castle Mouse (Figure 7-18) is a wonderful logic game created by Gabriel Jensen. The object of the game is to scare the mouse into his hole by placing the available animals on the chessboard-like playing surface. Of course, it's not as easy as it looks — there is a predatorial hierarchy at work here. A cat scares the mouse, a dog scares a cat, a polar bear scares a dog, a

Figure 7-19. The use of 1-bit graphics gives each of *Castle Mouse's* 10 levels (shown here) its own unique look.

Shockwave Studio

lion scares a polar bear, an elephant scares a lion, and lastly, the mouse scares an elephant. The object of the game is to place the animals at the bottom of the castle on the game board, positioning them in such a way that they will scare or be scared by the animals already in play and ultimately steer the mouse into his cozy hole. Each subsequent level offers a more challenging puzzle.

Using 1-bit graphics, Gabriel was able to create a unique look for each new level (Figure 7-19), while reusing the same set of 1-bit graphics. Let's look at how this was done.

Director offers a unique feature for adding interest to these diminutive graphics. You can quickly and easily color any 1-bit cast member with the Foreground color selector in the *Tool* palette.

Simply select a 1-bit cast member in the score (Figure 7-20) and choose a color from the foreground color selector. While limited in affecting the look of a single graphic, when combined with several layers of 1-bit graphics, this technique creates an impressive cumulative effect.

The colored chessboard in *Castle Mouse* is constructed of four separate 1-bit cast members, all of which are colored and combined to create a beveled, dimensional look to the board. Let's look at how these four cast members combine to make up the green beveled board of level 1.

Figure 7-20. The 1-bit graphics that make up *Castle Mouse's* game board (sprite channels 2–5) are layered on top of the 8-bit castle art in sprite channel 1.

In each of the figures on the following two pages, the large graphic shows the stage as each layer is added; the smaller graphic shows what each graphic looks like before it is colored; and where applicable, the third graphic shows the color chip chosen for each 1-bit graphic.

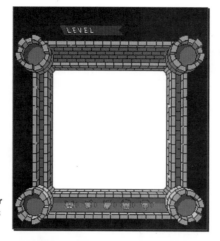

Figure 7-21. The first layer of the *Castle Mouse* art is this 8-bit graphic.

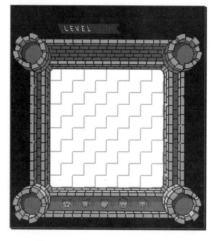

Figure 7-22. The next graphic is colored gray to act as a shadow bevel for the white squares.

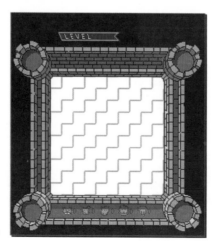

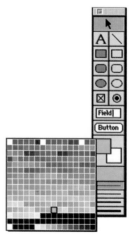

Figure 7-23. Next the highlight graphic for the colored squares is added.

Shockwave Studio

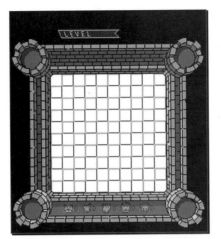
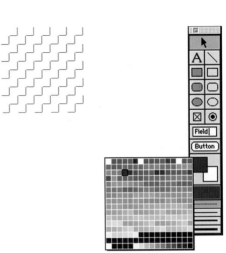

Figure 7-24. Next the shadow bevel for the colored squares is added.

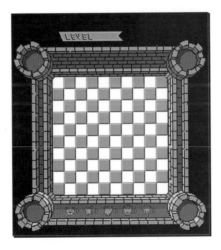

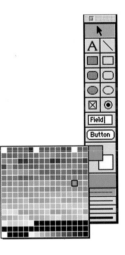

Figure 7-25. Then the colored squares are added.

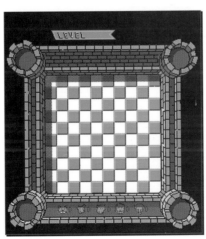
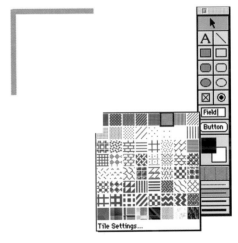

Figure 7-26. Finally two rectangle shapes, filled with a dot pattern, are added to create the shadow effect.

The first layer of *Castle Mouse* is the castle art itself (Figure 7-21). This 8-bit graphic is placed in sprite channel 1. Next, in sprite channel 2 is the first of the 1-bit graphics (Figure 7-22). This graphic is colored gray to act as the shadow bevel for the white squares. On top of this layer, in sprite channel 3, is a light green-colored 1-bit graphic (Figure 7-23), which is the highlight bevel for the green squares. In sprite channel 4 is the shadow bevel for the green squares. This is the third of the 1-bit graphics and it's been colored dark green (Figure 7-24). The final layer of the chessboard, in sprite channel 5, completes the effect with solid squares colored a medium green (Figure 7-25).

The remaining shadow effect (seen in Figure 7-26) is then added using two rectangles created with the *Tool* palette and filled with one of Director's built-in patterns.

As you can see, when used creatively, all of these techniques (1-bit graphics, tiled backgrounds, blending techniques, and ink effects) can greatly enhance your Shockwave movies while keeping the byte size very small.

8

Avoiding Problems with Palettes

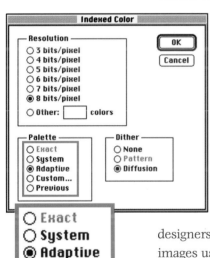

Figure 8-1. Adobe Photoshop's *Indexed Color* dialog box.

Color palettes are perhaps the single most perplexing issue facing Shockwave designers. With CD-ROM-based multimedia, designers can customize art and palettes for specific platforms. On the Web, you must create art that looks good (or at least acceptable) on both Windows and Macintosh and on various browsers.

While there isn't one universal answer to cover all graphics and all situations, understanding how color palettes work and how browsers use these palettes will give designers the ammunition they need to go out and fight their own palette battles.

Indexed images

Eight-bit color is essentially the common denominator for most computer platforms. Most computers in use today can handle 8-bit color and the goal for Web designers is to create images that work well in 8-bit. Eight-bit images use colors assigned to them in a color palette or index. For this reason, they are often referred to as indexed color images. Graphics with more than eight bits aren't subject to this restriction; they have the full gamut of 24-bit RGB color available to them.

When reducing an image's color depth from 24-bit to 8-bit or less, the designer is faced with several choices for creating the color palette. These options are described well in Adobe Photoshop's *Indexed Color* dialog box (Figure 8-1).

24-bit master

System palette

Adaptive palette

Custom palette
(216-color Netscape palette)

Figure 8-2. The various palette options.

For a comparison of these various palette options applied to an image, see Figure 8-2.

The first option, *Exact* is available only when the graphic already contains 256 colors or fewer. In this case, the color palette can contain the exact colors in the image.

System truncates the colors of the image to your computer platform's system palette.

The *Adaptive* palette option examines the image and creates a palette of the most used colors in the image, shifting or *dithering* the rest to those colors. (We'll discuss dithering shortly.) This method nearly always produces the best looking image.

The *Custom* option allows you to load a pre-existing palette.

And finally, *Previous* will use the same palette used on the last image you indexed. This is an easy way to apply the same palette to a series of images.

The super palette

So which palette to use? It's not always an easy decision even with a single image. In a multimedia or Web project where many images are used, the problem is compounded by the fact that each individual graphic can have its own color palette.

On an 8-bit system, only one of these palettes can be displayed at a time on the screen, usually that of the first graphic displayed. All other graphics on the screen are forced into this one palette, which can produce some very unpredictable results. Similarly, all the graphics in any single frame of a Director movie must have the same palette; if they don't, they will be forced under the current active palette.

One solution is to use a *super palette* — a palette that includes the most commonly used colors from a series of images, not just one image. A super palette is a single consistent palette that you can use for all images in all frames.

Its only drawback is that as each image is added to the palette, more and more color information has to be factored in, thus reducing the color accuracy of any one image (see Figure 8-3). If the images all have widely diverging color schemes, each image will suffer more from having only a portion of the available colors applied to it. This can cause severe dithering.

The basics of color

The basic essence of online graphics is the bitmap. A bitmap is essentially a grid, or map, of pixels that make up and define an image. The resolution or quality of a bitmap is measured in two ways: spatial resolution, or fineness of the bitmap, and color resolution, or depth of the bitmap.

Spatial resolution is measured in the physical number of pixels in an image, and is usually expressed in pixels per inch (ppi). The finer the spatial resolution, the bigger the file size of the image will be. For example, a 300 ppi image, typical of those used in printing, at 8" x 10" would have a file size upwards of 20 megabytes. This high-resolution is necessary to achieve the desired output on film, plates, and eventually the printing press. However, because the final output of a multimedia project is the computer screen, the resolution can be much lower. Low-resolution images — often referred to as screen-resolution images — are typically 72 ppi, which is the resolution of Macintosh monitors. The smaller the spatial resolution, the smaller the file size.

The enlarged area of this example shows the bitmap that creates the curve of the letter B.

Spatial resolution in Director

Because Macromedia Director was initially a Mac-only program, graphics must be 72 ppi before being imported into Director's cast or they will be resized, depending on their spatial resolution.

Before importing into Director		After importing into Director	
Pixel dimensions	ppi	size in inches	pixel dimensions
216 x 216	72	3" x 3"	216 x 216
216 x 216	150	1.444" x 1.444"	104 x 104
216 x 216	300	.722" x .722"	52 x 52

As you can see, a 216 x 216 pixel graphic at 72 pixels per inch would import into Director at the correct screen size of 3" x 3". But when the same pixel-size graphic is at a resolution of 300 ppi, it imports into Director at the much smaller size of less than ¾ of an inch.

Color depth, the second way in which resolution is measured, is discussed in the sidebar, "There's low res, and then there's Web res."

Adaptive palette

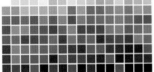

Super palette

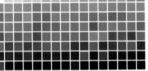

Figure 8-3. In this example you can see the effects of dithering as more color information is factored into the super palette. The adaptive palette (top) includes only colors taken from the image of the grandfather and grandson fishing. This palette produces little dithering as seen in the inset circle to the right of the palette. The super palette (bottom) factors in colors from the other two photos and produces the more severe dithering and loss of detail, as seen in the inset circle to the right.

Therefore, it is important to plan your project carefully to create images that all have similar color schemes.

Making super palettes with Debabelizer

Next to Director and Photoshop, Debabelizer from Equilibrium is probably the multimedia designer's best friend. For years, creating a super palette on the Macintosh has been a breeze with Debabelizer. And, finally, a Windows version of Debabelizer is now available. Debabelizer offers multimedia designers excellent handling of palette reduction, the ability to batch-process images, and, most importantly, the ability to easily create a super palette.

Let's look at how to make a super palette in Debabelizer 1.6.5 for the Macintosh.

First select *File/Batch/Super Palette.* This brings up the dialog box seen in Figure 8-4. The first step in creating the super palette is to create a batch list of all the images you want to include in the palette. To do this, click the *New* button. This brings up the dialog box in Figure 8-5.

Shockwave Studio

There's low res, and then there's Web res

For Shockwave designers, color depth is a much more important consideration than spatial resolution.

Each pixel in an image's bitmap contains color information that is referred to as its bit depth or color depth. The color depth of the image determines the possible number of colors available for each pixel. Each bit can have one of two states — on or off. For example, a 1-bit image can have two possible colors, white (on) or black (off). One of the most common bit depths found in color monitors is 8-bit, which allows 256 possible colors (2^8). This is why so many multimedia projects are typically 8-bit. As you can see in the chart below, as the bit depth rises, the number of colors increases exponentially.

Color depth	Possible colors	Exponent
1	2	2^1
2	4	2^2
3	8	2^3
4	16	2^4
5	32	2^5
6	64	2^6
7	128	2^7
8	256	2^8
16	65,536	2^{16}
24	16,777,216	2^{24}

Just as with spatial resolution, the smaller the color depth, the smaller the final file size will be. On the Web this can be a very important issue for people with limited bandwidth modems. You may have to make sacrifices on the number of colors you use in your graphics in order to trim down the file sizes of your movies. You may have a beautiful Shockwave movie with 24-bit graphics, but those graphics, beautiful or not, won't do any good if nobody waits long enough for it to download. When designing graphics for *Web Review* magazine, this is always one of our conscious design limitations; all graphics have to be 5-bit or less, many of them are 3-bit — a mere 8 colors!

Debabelizer

For information on how to obtain Debabelizer, see Equilibrium's Web site at: *http://www.equilibrium.com/.*

In the left window, find the folder that contains the images you want to include in the super palette. To add the images to the *Batch List* in the right window, click *Append All.* Once you have all the images you wish to include in the super palette entered in the *Batch List* window, name the list in the *Batch List Name* window in the lower-right corner and click *Save.*

This takes you back to the *Batch SuperPalette* dialog box (Figure 8-4). Your *Batch List* is now displayed in the window on the left. Select the *Call It* radio button in the right column and give your palette a name. Next, choose the number of colors you want in the super palette. In this example, I've chosen 128 colors. Click *Do It* to create the super palette. Each image is automatically opened — one by one — and figured into the super palette. When Debabelizer is finished, the *Create Super Palette* dialog box comes up (Figure 8-6).

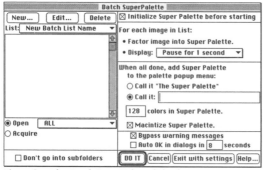

Figure 8-4. The *Batch SuperPalette* dialog box.

Figure 8-5. The *Batch List* window.

Shockwave Studio

This series of images is taken from a Shockwave movie I created for Nokia and is an excellent example of the use of super palettes. Although all the images look similar, because of the rotation of the phone, each image had slightly different lighting. Rather than forcing all the images into the palette of one of the other images, I was able to create a super palette that worked with all the images by using Debabelizer. You can see the Nokia phone in action at *http://www.nokia-asia.com/ap/9000_shock.html.*

In this dialog box, you can check all your settings again. After verifying the settings, click *Create It.* Now the super palette can be applied to your images. Open an image, and select **Palette/Set Palette & Remap Pixels.** This brings up the dialog box seen in Figure 8-7. From the **Set Palette** pop-up menu, select your newly created super palette. For the best results, select *Remap Pixels* and *Dither when remapping.* To apply the super palette to the image, click *OK.*

Making super palettes in Photoshop

You can also make a super palette using Adobe Photoshop (available for both Mac and Windows). Creating a super palette in Photoshop is as easy as making a new document large enough to fit all of the images for which you're creating the super palette. Then simply paste each graphic into the document as seen in

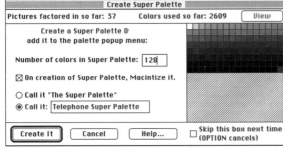

Figure 8-6. The *Create Super Palette* dialog box.

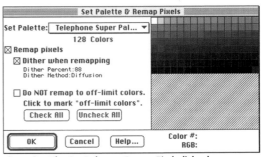

Figure 8-7. The *Set Palette & Remap Pixels* dialog box.

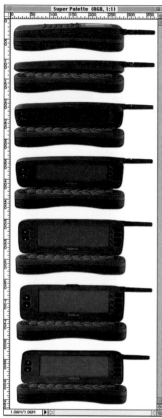

Figure 8-8. A super palette can also be created in Photoshop by pasting the images into one file and selecting the *Adaptive* palette option in the *Indexed Color* dialog box.

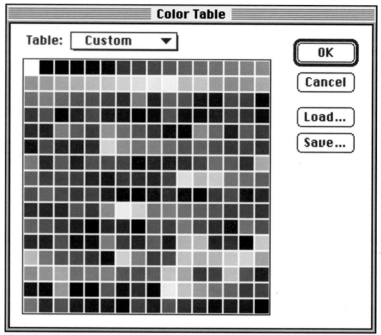

Figure 8-9. Photoshop's *Color Table* dialog box shows the newly created super palette for the series of images in Figure 8-8.

Figure 8-8. After this, select **Mode/Indexed Color** and select the *Adaptive* palette option. Select the number of colors you want to include in your super palette and click *OK*.

Next, select **Mode/Color Table.** This brings up the new palette of the composite image (Figure 8-9), essentially a super palette for all the images. At this point, you can edit the individual colors of the color table, if you feel it's necessary, to improve the quality of the graphics. After you have the palette you want, simply click *Save* to save the palette.

You can then use this palette for each individual image by opening the image and converting it to *Indexed Color* mode. In the *Indexed Color* dialog box, choose custom palette and then load your new super palette. Clicking *OK* in the *Indexed Color* dialog box applies the palette to the image.

Application palettes

Just as each individual 8-bit image has its own color palette, so does each application operating under a monitor bit depth of

8-bits. On the Macintosh, there's a built-in 8-bit system palette; on 8-bit Macs (or applications running at 8-bit) the Mac system palette defines the colors that are available. In Windows, each application has its own distinct color palette — all graphics are truncated to the colors of this palette, whatever it may be. This creates a perplexing problem for Web designers. Which palette can they use that will allow all their graphics to look good on multiple platforms and different monitor bit depths?

Fortunately for Web designers, all popular Windows browsers use the same 216-color palette while in 8-bit mode (Figure 8-10). Commonly referred to as the Netscape palette, this palette's colors were culled from the Macintosh 256-color system palette (Figure 8-11). This makes it possible to design graphics that work on both platforms in 8-bit mode. The downside to the palette is that the colors aren't all that great. Still, by creating art that uses these browser-safe colors as their base set of colors, you can be assured of graphics that will look decent on both platforms in 8-bit-color mode.

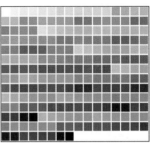

Figure 8-10. The browser-safe palette. This palette is used in Window's browsers operating in 8-bit color mode. The palette is made up of the first 216 colors of the Macintosh system palette.

The Netscape browser-safe palette

This palette uses only six different values to describe the 216 colors for use in Windows. The RGB values of these colors are: 0, 51, 102, 153, 204, and 255. All the colors of the browser-safe palette are made up of red, green, and blue combinations of these six values. You can enter these values directly into the color picker of an image editing program such as Adobe Photoshop and use them in your graphics (Figure 8-12).

How browsers work

On Macs running in 8-bit mode, browsers use the Mac system palette to display colors. Any colors not in the Mac palette are simulated as closely as possible by dithering two or more of the colors in the palette to create an approximation of the color. Dithering is similar to the color halftones used in printing, where color dots are combined to simulate a wide variety of different colors.

Windows machines running in 8-bit mode use the 216-color, browser-safe palette described above and dither or shift all colors outside this palette. By using this color palette as a basis for

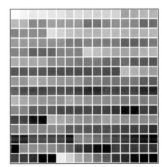

Figure 8-11. The Macintosh system palette. This palette is used on Macs running in 8-bit color mode. If you compare this palette to the one in Figure 8-10, you'll notice both are the same, except this palette has an additional 40 colors.

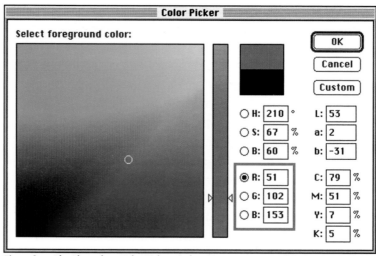

Figure 8-12. The Photoshop *Color Picker* window. You can use any of the browser-safe colors in your graphics by entering any combination of 0, 51, 102, 153, 204, or 255 in the RGB spaces (outlined in red).

The Netscape palette is included on the CD-ROM in PICT format for import into Director. Import *samples/palette.pic*, on your CD, into the cast of your Director movie. When the *Image Options* dialog box comes up, under *Color Depth* select *Import*. This will import the palette of the image into the cast and make it available for use in the palette channel.

creating your art, you can rest assured that you won't have any severe dithering or color shifts on 8-bit systems of either platform.

Using palettes in Director

When importing indexed images into Director, you are presented with several options (Figure 8-13). Your first choice is *Color Depth*. You can choose either the image's color depth (8-bit or less) or the 32-bit stage. If you import at the image's color depth, you must choose which palette to use. The *Import* option brings the indexed image's palette into the Director movie's cast. You may also choose to remap the image to any of Director's built-in palettes or another palette in the cast. When remapping, you can

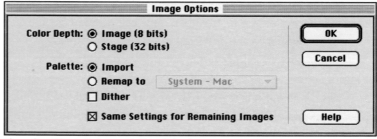

Figure 8-13. Director's *Image Options* dialog box.

also choose to dither the image or not. If you are importing a lot of images at once, select *Same Settings for Remaining Images* to apply these settings to all the images.

Once a palette is in the cast it can then be used in the palette channel of the movie's score (Figure 8-14). Placing the palette in the palette channel forces all the images in that frame to that palette, so make sure that all images within the frame use that common palette.

By double-clicking on the palette channel in any given frame, you can bring up the *Frame Properties: Palette* dialog box (Figure 8-15). This box allows you to set the palette for that frame to any of Director's built-in palettes or any palette imported into the cast. If you choose the *Palette Transition* option under *Action,* it will create a smooth transition between two frames with different palettes by blending between the two palettes. You can also choose to fade the palette transition to black or white by choosing one of the radio buttons under *Options.*

The *Color Cycling* option cycles the palette through the colors selected in the palette at the left. This can be used to create some very interesting effects, but will play havoc with the browser window and desktop colors of the user's computer. Color cycling only works if the user's monitor is set to 8-bit.

The *Rate* option determines the speed of the transition.

The following pages show samples of various palette configurations and their effects on different platforms at different color depths.

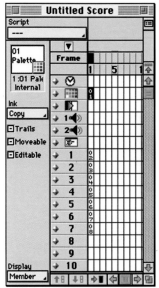

Figure 8-14. Director's score window with a custom palette loaded into the palette channel.

Figure 8-15. The *Frame Properties: Palette* dialog box.

Monitor color depth: 24-bit
Cast color depth: 24-bit
Stage color depth: 24-bit
Palette attribute: background
DCR file size: 271 K

Monitor color depth: 24-bit
Cast color depth: 7-bit palette
Stage color depth: 24-bit
Palette attribute: background
DCR file size: 144 K

Monitor color depth: 24-bit
Cast color depth: 7-bit palette
Stage color depth: 7-bit palette
Palette attribute: background
DCR file size: 95 K

Monitor color depth: 24-bit
Cast color depth: 7-bit palette
Stage color depth: Mac palette
Palette attribute: background
DCR file size: 95 K

Monitor color depth: 8-bit
Cast color depth: 7-bit palette
Stage color depth: 24-bit
Palette attribute: background
DCR file size: 144 K

Monitor color depth: 8-bit
Cast color depth: 7-bit palette
Stage color depth: 24-bit
Palette attribute: foreground
DCR file size: 144 K

Monitor color depth: 8-bit
Cast color depth: 7-bit palette
Stage color depth: 7-bit palette
Palette attribute: background
DCR file size: 95 K

Monitor color depth: 8-bit
Cast color depth: 7-bit palette
Stage color depth: 7-bit palette
Palette attribute: foreground
DCR file size: 95 K

Monitor color depth: 8-bit
Cast color depth: NS palette✲✲
Stage color depth: NS palette✲✲
Palette attribute: background
DCR file size: 83 K

Monitor color depth: 8-bit
Cast color depth: NS palette✲✲
Stage color depth: NS palette✲✲
Palette attribute: foreground
DCR file size: 83 K

Monitor color depth: 8-bit
Cast color depth: 24-bit
Stage color depth: 24-bit
Palette attribute: background
DCR file size: 271 K

Monitor color depth: 8-bit
Cast color depth: 24-bit
Stage color depth: 24-bit
Palette attribute: foreground
DCR file size: 271 K

✲Director's built-in Windows palette   ✲✲216-color browser-safe Netscape palette

Monitor color depth: 24-bit
Cast color depth: 7-bit palette
Stage color depth: Win palette*
Palette attribute: background
DCR file size: 95 K

Monitor color depth: 24-bit
Cast color depth: NS palette**
Stage color depth: NS palette**
Palette attribute: background
DCR file size: 83 K

Monitor color depth: 8-bit
Cast color depth: 24-bit
Stage color depth: 24-bit
Palette attribute: background
DCR file size: 271 K

Monitor color depth: 8-bit
Cast color depth: 24-bit
Stage color depth: 24-bit
Palette attribute: foreground
DCR file size: 271 K

Monitor color depth: 8-bit
Cast color depth: 7-bit palette
Stage color depth: Mac palette
Palette attribute: background
DCR file size: 95 K

Monitor color depth: 8-bit
Cast color depth: 7-bit palette
Stage color depth: Mac palette
Palette attribute: foreground
DCR file size: 95 K

Monitor color depth: 8-bit
Cast color depth: 7-bit palette
Stage color depth: Win palette*
Palette attribute: background
DCR file size: 95 K

Monitor color depth: 8-bit
Cast color depth: 7-bit palette
Stage color depth: Win palette*
Palette attribute: foreground
DCR file size: 95 K

Monitor color depth: 8-bit
Cast color depth: 7-bit palette
Stage color depth: 24-bit
Palette attribute: background
DCR file size: 144 K

Monitor color depth: 8-bit
Cast color depth: 7-bit palette
Stage color depth: 24-bit
Palette attribute: foreground
DCR file size: 144 K

Monitor color depth: 8-bit
Cast color depth: 7-bit palette
Stage color depth: 7-bit palette
Palette attribute: background
DCR file size: 95 K

Monitor color depth: 8-bit
Cast color depth: 7-bit palette
Stage color depth: 7-bit palette
Palette attribute: foreground
DCR file size: 95 K

Avoiding Problems with Palettes

Monitor color depth: 8-bit
Cast color depth: 7-bit palette
Stage color depth: Mac palette
Palette attribute: background
DCR file size: 95 K

Monitor color depth: 8-bit
Cast color depth: 7-bit palette
Stage color depth: Mac palette
Palette attribute: foreground
DCR file size: 95 K

Monitor color depth: 8-bit
Cast color depth: 7-bit palette
Stage color depth: Win palette☆
Palette attribute: background
DCR file size: 95 K

Monitor color depth: 8-bit
Cast color depth: 7-bit palette
Stage color depth: Win palette☆
Palette attribute: foreground
DCR file size: 95 K

Monitor color depth: 8-bit
Cast color depth: NS palette☆☆
Stage color depth: NS palette☆☆
Palette attribute: background
DCR file size: 83 K

Monitor color depth: 8-bit
Cast color depth: NS palette☆☆
Stage color depth: NS palette☆☆
Palette attribute: foreground
DCR file size: 83 K

Using the *palette* attribute

The *EMBED* tag allows you to control the palette that Shockwave will use with the *palette* attribute. (Remember that you use the *EMBED* tag to place a Shockwave movie in HTML. For more information on the *EMBED* tag, see Appendix A.) The attribute *palette* = "*foreground*" forces the browser to use your movie's palette instead of the browser's palette.

There are several drawbacks to doing this. First and foremost is that all the other graphics and Shockwave movies on the page are subject to the palette of the first movie loaded. Also, because applications like Netscape only use 216 colors, they don't interfere with the colors used by the Windows system; replacing the application palette with a custom 256-color palette causes the colors of the Windows desktop and interface elements to shift, sometimes with bizarre results.

Which palette is best?

When comparing the image quality and file sizes of the examples on the preceeding pages, you will see that there is no one best answer to the question of which palette to use. However, it is clear that some ways are much better than others! As you would expect, using the Netscape palette with the palette attribute set to background (the browser's palette is used) yields the best results across both platforms and monitor bit-depths. It also produced the smallest file size, although the quality of the art does suffer compared to the 24-bit and adaptive palette versions. You'll have to decide which combination of file size, image quality, and cross-platform compatibility is acceptable to you. Hopefully this comparison will help make the choice easier, but the best answer will come from your own experimentation.

The best advice for Shockwave designers is:

- Stick to colors in or close to the Netscape palette.
- Always test on multiple platforms early in the project.

Keep these simple rules in mind, and you should be able to achieve very good results on both platforms.

Now let's look at another way you can use palettes within Director: by matching the color of the stage with the background color of your Web page.

Matching backgrounds

In HTML, you can control the background color of your page with the *BODY BGCOLOR* tag. By using the same color in the *BODY* tag as you do in the background of your stage, you can seamlessly integrate your Shockwave movie onto your Web page.

A typical *BODY* statement looks like this:

```
<BODY BGCOLOR="#ffffff">
```

The value "ffffff" is the hexadecimal equivalent of the RGB values 255, 255, and 255 — which is pure white. The hexadecimal system is a base-16 system, as opposed to the base-10 system that Photoshop uses to display RGB values. In order to use RGB values from Photoshop as a *BGCOLOR,* they must first be converted to hexadecimal, which is a six-character set as in the example above. The first two characters represent the red value, the next two characters green, and the last set of two represents the blue value. The hexadecimal equivalents of the values in the Netscape palette are 00, 33, 66, 99, CC, and FF (Figure 8-16). Using combinations of these values will produce the colors of the Netscape palette in the background of your Web page. But, what if you want to use a color not in the Netscape palette for a background color? Let's look at how to convert decimal to hexadecimal.

Browser-safe values

Decimal	Hexadecimal
0	00
51	33
102	66
153	99
204	CC
255	FF

Figure 8-16. Decimal and hexadecimal values for the colors in the Netscape palette.

When does 25 equal 19? When it's hexadecimal.

To convert a red, green, or blue value to hexadecimal, you must first divide the value by 16, subtract the integer (this becomes the first value of the two-character set) and multiply the remainder by 16 for the second value. Confused? Well it's actually very simple, let's look at an example.

Let's take the RGB value from Photoshop's Picker shown in Figure 8-17. First, we'll start with the red value of 212. Divide 212 by 16 and you get 13.25. Thirteen is the first value of the two-character set, but because we are dealing with the base-16 hexadecimal system, 13 equals D (Figure 8-18). Next, take the remainder (.25) and multiply it by 16. You should get a value of four. So, the RGB value of 212, in Photoshop, equals D4 in hexadecimal. Now, repeat the steps for the other two values. You'll end up with D4 for red, 9F for green, and 55 for blue. Put D49F55 in the *BODY* tag and your Web page will be the same color as the brown shown in the Photoshop color picker.

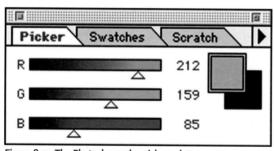

Figure 8-17. The Photoshop color picker palette.

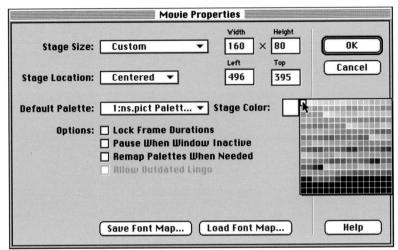

Figure 8-19. The *Movie Properties* dialog box.

Base-10	Base-16
0	0
1	1
2	2
3	3
4	4
5	5
6	6
7	7
8	8
9	9
10	A
11	B
12	C
13	D
14	E
15	F

Figure 8-18. Base-16 equivalents for the numbers 0–15.

Changing stage colors

The final step is to match the color of the stage to the background color of your Web page. You will first need to import your palette into the movie's cast as described in the previous section, "Using palettes in Director." Then, to set the color of the stage, select **Modify/Movie/Properties.** This brings up the *Movie Properties* dialog box as shown in Figure 8-19. From the *Default Palette* pop-up menu, select the palette you just imported. Under the *Stage Color* pop-up menu, select the color you want for the stage color.

You will find that planning your palette early on in your project and using that palette for all aspects of your design — from the Shockwave movie to the graphics to the colors on the page — will save you a mountain of headaches in the end.

9 Using Net-Specific Lingo

When the Lingo language was first created, nobody at Macromedia could perceive the need for any functions that would reach beyond the desktop. With the advent of Shockwave, they knew they were going to have to extend the Lingo language to take advantage of many of the Internet's unique features — things like calling a URL or fetching text from a server halfway around the world. Thankfully, because of the extensible nature of Lingo, Macromedia was able to add many new Net-specific Lingo commands. In this chapter we'll learn many of these commands by looking at several real-world examples.

Netscape: multi maze

Location: http://www.luna.nl/~mare/e/maze.html

Go to my shockwave page.

multi maze is a combination of a maze and a "hot wire" game. Grab the ball and drag it to the red hole, without touching the maze wall. If you touch the walls you will return to your previous starting position and lose one of your six lives. The same happens if you rest and release the mousebutton.
multi maze is part of a series of mazegames on different sites on the Internet. When you've reached the last hole you have access to another mazegame, somewhere else on the World Wide Web.
Have fun

multi maze

part of the
world wide
maze

help   start

The full version of Mark's *multi maze* can be played at *http://www.luna.nl/~mare/e/maze.html*

An amazing web of mazes

Tucked snugly between Germany and the North Sea lies the Netherlands and a man with a puzzling vision. Mark Reijners has a vision of a world populated with Shockwave puzzle mazes all linked together by the Web. Solving one maze leads to another maze — at a different location on the Web, possibly half a world away — and then to another maze ... a virtually endless maze of mazes, bringing together the far corners of the Internet.

Now you can join the fun and link your site to the chain by creating your own maze and in the process learn how to use some of Shockwave's Net-specific Lingo, the commands that let Shockwave

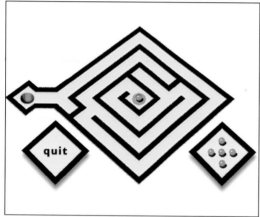

Figure 9-1. The multi maze consists of three main screens: the opening screen (top), the maze screen and a go-to-the-next-level screen.

movies connect to HTML pages, talk to Web servers and retain specific user information.

The *multi maze*

On the CD-ROM that accompanies this book, (at *source/maze.dir*) you'll find a sample maze provided by Mark. Though we don't have the space to describe all of the code in the maze — some of it you'll have to discover on your own — we'll look at the main workings here.

The maze is comprised of three main screens (Figure 9-1), an opening screen, the maze, and a next-level screen. Each of these screens perform an important function which we will look at one by one.

Last things first: preloading the next maze

The first thing the maze does, after the user downloads it, is to immediately begin preloading the next maze to which the user will be sent once this maze is solved. Let's look at how this works.

The first screen the maze player sees is the opening screen. Although this screen seems straightforward enough, beneath the surface something very important is going on. In addition to providing navigational buttons that link to a help screen and the maze screen, this first screen is preparing to go to the next maze by randomly selecting a maze from a list retrieved from the Internet and preloading it into the browser's cache.

When the movie starts, even before we get to this opening screen, a custom handler named *loadlevelstext* (Figure 9-2) is called. (This handler will load a text file containing a list of URLs for other mazes around the Internet.)

The first line of code **Ⓐ** initializes a global variable called *gVisitedLevelsList*. This is a list that will keep track of all the mazes the user has

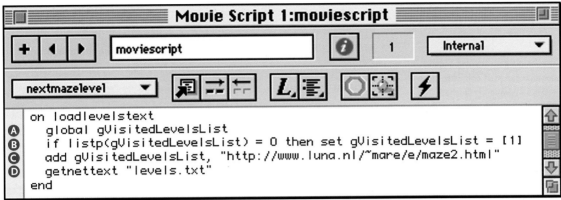

Figure 9-2. The *loadlevelstext* handler loads a text file containing a list of other mazes on the Internet.

visited in this session. Because it is a global variable, the values it contains persist from movie to movie. The next line **ⓑ** checks to see if the variable is in fact a list, and if not it makes it a list. Line **ⓒ** adds the current maze's URL to this list.

The last line of the handler **ⓓ** uses one of Shockwave's special Net-specific Lingo commands, *getNetText*. The *getNetText* command simply grabs the text of a file on the Internet and brings it into the Shockwave movie. In this case, we're calling for a text document called *levels.txt* that resides in the same directory as the Shockwave movie. This text document contains the URLs of all the other mazes around the Internet. For each maze in the *levels.txt* document there are two entries: the URL of the maze movie itself and the URL of the HTML page that contains the movie, for example:

```
http://www.luna.nl/~mare/sw/movmaze.dcr
http://www.luna.nl/~mare/e/maze2.html

http://www.luna.nl/~mare/sw/multimaze.dcr
http://www.luna.nl/~mare/e/maze.html

http://www.luna.nl/~salabim/sw/memmaze.dcr
http://www.luna.nl/~salabim/e/maze3.html
```

After this start-up script work is executed, the movie moves to the frame with the opening screen. In this frame an *exitFrame* script calls another custom handler named *nextmazelevel* (Figure 9-3). This handler randomly chooses the next maze to go to and preloads it into memory. Let's look at the script.

Lingo tip

One of the simplest ways to accomplish intermovie communication is through the use of global variables. These variables will persist from movie to movie allowing you to pass information from one to another.

For a complete list of Shockwave's Net-specific Lingo, see Appendix B.

Mark Reijners' Web site is located at: *http://www.luna.nl/~mare/*

The first line **Ⓐ** initializes several global variables. The next line **Ⓑ** checks to see if the *getNetText* operation, begun in the *loadLevelsText* script, is finished. It uses the *NetDone* command, another Net-specific command, which checks the progress of asynchronous network operations such as *getNetText, preLoadNetThing, gotoNetMovie* or *gotoNetPage.* This is important to check, as the results of the *getNetText* command cannot be used until the operation is concluded. *NetDone* returns *TRUE* when the operation is complete.

Asynchronous means that another operation can start only after the previous operation is finished.

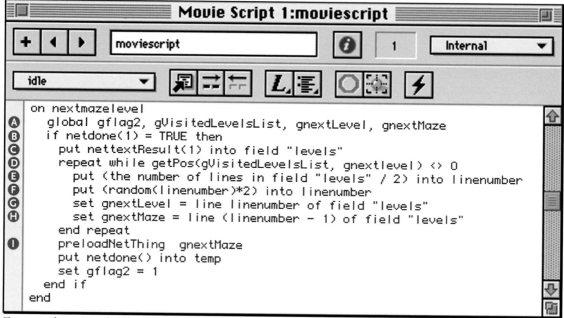

```
on nextmazelevel
   global gflag2, gVisitedLevelsList, gnextLevel, gnextMaze
   if netdone(1) = TRUE then
      put nettextResult(1) into field "levels"
      repeat while getPos(gVisitedLevelsList, gnextlevel) <> 0
         put (the number of lines in field "levels" / 2) into linenumber
         put (random(linenumber)*2) into linenumber
         set gnextLevel = line linenumber of field "levels"
         set gnextMaze = line (linenumber - 1) of field "levels"
      end repeat
      preloadNetThing  gnextMaze
      put netdone() into temp
      set gflag2 = 1
   end if
end
```

Figure 9-3. The *nextmazelevel* handler randomly chooses the next maze and preloads it into memory.

Once the *getNetText* operation is concluded, the results are put into a text field called *levels.* **Ⓒ** This is done with the Net-specific Lingo, *netTextResult.*

Next, the script uses a *repeat* loop to pick the next maze at random. The first line of the repeat loop **Ⓓ** ensures that the current maze won't be picked as the next maze. Let's look at how this is accomplished.

Remember, there are two URL entries for each maze listed in the text file, which is now in the field called *levels.* In order for

Shockwave Studio

the script to pick a maze at random, it needs to know how many actual mazes there are in the list. Since each maze consists of two URL entries, the script divides the number of entries in the *levels* field by 2, and puts the result in a local variable called *linenumber*. ❺ This produces a number equal to the actual number of mazes in the list.

In our example there were three mazes listed in the *levels* text, each with two entries, for a total of six entries. So in this example, the value contained in *linenumber* would equal 3.

The next line ❻ picks a random number between 1 and the value of *linenumber,* multiplies it by 2 (to find its actual place in the *levels* text) and makes this number the new value of *linenumber.* So, for example, if the random number picked by the handler is 2, the resulting value in *linenumber* would be 4.

In the next line of code, the value of *linenumber* is used to choose a line from *levels,* which is put into a global variable called *gnextLevel.* ❼ The next line ❽ puts the entry at the previous position in the *levels* field into another variable called *gnextMaze.* In our example, *linenumber* equals 4, so the fourth line from *levels* is used for *gnextLevel* and the third line is used for *gnextMaze.* In the end, *gnextLevel* contains the URL for the HTML page of the next level, and *gnextMaze* contains the URL for the Shockwave movie for the next level. The URL in *gnextLevel* will come into play later in the movie, but the URL in *gnextMaze* is used in the next line.

The Net-specific Lingo *preloadNetThing* ❿ preloads the Shockwave movie at the URL contained in *gnextMaze* into the browser's cache file. Once this preload sequence is started, the user can jump to the maze screen by clicking on the *Start* button.

Figure 9-4. The final screen of the *multi maze.*

Figure 9-a. The three layers that make up the maze. Note that the ball, the green starting dot and the red ending hole are separate cast members (inset).

Figure 9-b. The assembled maze.

Through the maze

Though the actual workings of the maze aren't related to Net-specific Lingo, they are interesting to the Shockwave author nevertheless. In Chapter 6 we created a slider by constraining one graphic within another. The *multi maze* project uses a similar technique to constrain the movement of the ball through a more complex shape. In this sidebar we'll discuss how the maze is created and the Lingo that is used to constrain the ball to the inside of the maze.

Constructing the maze

The maze has six distinct parts, the ball, the green starting dot, the black maze walls, the yellow maze interior, the light yellow background, and the finish hole. Notice, in Figure 9-a, how the three layers that make up the maze stack on top of each other to make up the final maze shown in Figure 9-b.

The maze works by using the bright yellow graphic as a constraining shape. This graphic defines the boundaries of the maze. As the user drags the ball through the maze, the game checks to make sure the mouse doesn't stray from this graphic. If it does, the user loses one life and the ball goes back to its starting point. Let's take a look at the Lingo that makes this work.

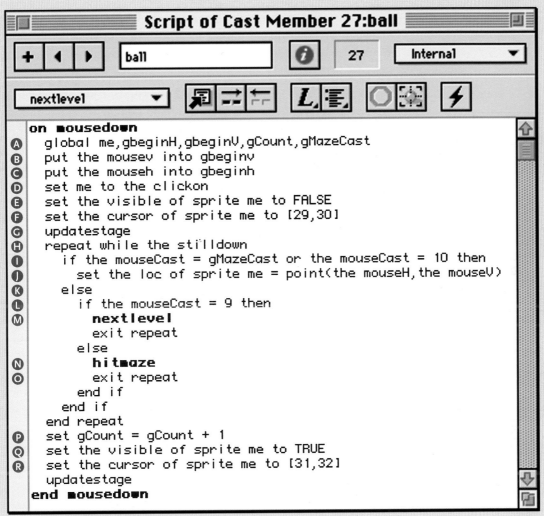

```
         Script of Cast Member 27:ball

  +  ◀  ▶   ball          ⓘ   27      Internal   ▼

  nextlevel        ▼  🗗 ⇄ ⇤  𝐿,≣  ○ ⊡ ⚡

     on mousedown
Ⓐ     global me,gbeginH,gbeginV,gCount,gMazeCast
Ⓑ     put the mousev into gbeginv
Ⓒ     put the mouseh into gbeginh
Ⓓ     set me to the clickon
Ⓔ     set the visible of sprite me to FALSE
Ⓕ     set the cursor of sprite me to [29,30]
Ⓖ     updatestage
Ⓗ     repeat while the stilldown
Ⓘ        if the mouseCast = gMazeCast or the mouseCast = 10 then
Ⓙ           set the loc of sprite me = point(the mouseH,the mouseV)
Ⓚ        else
Ⓛ           if the mouseCast = 9 then
Ⓜ              nextlevel
              exit repeat
           else
Ⓝ              hitmaze
Ⓞ              exit repeat
           end if
        end if
     end repeat
Ⓟ     set gCount = gCount + 1
Ⓠ     set the visible of sprite me to TRUE
Ⓡ     set the cursor of sprite me to [31,32]
     updatestage
     end mousedown
```

Figure 9-c. The *mouseDown* script that is attached to the ball.

When the user clicks on the ball, the movie calls the
mouseDown script attached to it (Figure 9-c). After initializing
several global variables, Ⓐ the script then puts the vertical and
horizontal positions of the mouse cursor into the variables
gbeginv and *gbeginh* Ⓑ Ⓒ respectively. This is done to preserve
the starting point of the ball when it is clicked on. If the user hits
the wall of the maze, the ball is set back to these coordinates.

Next, **D** the script puts the number of the sprite that was just clicked on (the ball) into a local variable called *me*. From that point on, whenever the script refers to *me*, it knows that it refers to the ball graphic. Using the variable in this way is an easy way of keeping track of a sprite. Next, **E** the ball is made invisible and the cursor is changed **F** to the hand holding the ball graphic (see Figure 9-d). The ball is made invisible to speed up the game play and make dragging the ball through the maze much smoother. After the script updates the stage to show the changes, **G** the script enters into a repeat loop that will last as long as the mouse is held down. **H**

Figure 9-d. The custom cursor.

This repeat loop uses *if...then* statements and the Lingo *mouseCast* to check if the user is still in the maze or has reached the end. The *mouseCast* command refers to the cast member that is directly under the mouse cursor's hot spot. The first *if...then* statement **I** checks to see if the mouse is over either the constraining graphic (the variable *gMazeCast* had been set earlier in the movie to contain the number of the bright yellow graphic) or over the green starting dot (cast member number 10). If so, it sets the location of the ball graphic *(me)* to the mouse location. **J**

If the ball is not over either the constraining graphic or the starting dot, it can mean only one of two things, either the user has reached the finish hole, or has hit the wall. With the *else* portion **K** of the *if...then* statement, the script first checks to see if the mouse is over the finish hole (cast member number 9). **L** If it is, the script runs a custom handler called *nextLevel*. **M** This handler sends the player on to the final *Congratulations* screen. If the mouse is not over the finish hole, it means the player hit the wall, so the script jumps to a handler called *hitmaze* **N** that will reset the ball to its previous position.

The *hitmaze* handler, seen in Figure 9-e, first initializes several global variables for use in this script. **A** Next, it sounds the system beep **B** of the user's computer. After that, it simply sets the location of the ball *(me)* to the location where the user first started dragging it. **C** Remember, *gbeginH* and *gbeginV* were set at the beginning of the *mouseDown* script for just this

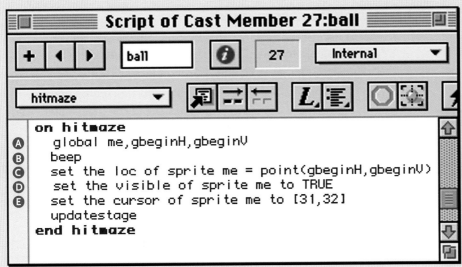

```
Script of Cast Member 27:ball

+  ◀  ▶    ball        ⓘ    27    Internal ▼

hitmaze        ▼  🔳 🔁 🔙  L 🔃  ◯ 🔳

    on hitmaze
(A)   global me,gbeginH,gbeginV
(B)   beep
(C)   set the loc of sprite me = point(gbeginH,gbeginV)
(D)   set the visible of sprite me to TRUE
(E)   set the cursor of sprite me to [31,32]
      updatestage
    end hitmaze
```

Figure 9-e. The *hitmaze* handler.

purpose. Next, the script turns the ball visible again **D** and changes the cursor back to the open hand. **E** The handler then ends and the movie returns to the *mouseDown* script at the point it left (Figure 9-c, **N**).

At this point, the *mouseDown* script exits the repeat loop **O** and executes the final few statements in the *mouseDown* handler. First, 1 is added to the variable called *gCount*. **P** This variable is used to keep track of the lives remaining in the game. We'll show how that works in a moment. Next, the ball is turned visible **Q** and the cursor for the ball is changed to the open hand. **R** If these commands seem to repeat the ones in the *hitmaze* handler, it's because they do. The reason for doing this is to account for the final option the user has. The user at any point can stop dragging the ball, leaving the ball at the point the user let up on the mouse and beginning again from that point. Doing so costs one life and is also the reason for the final two lines of code. Once the user clicks on the ball again, the *mouseDown* script starts over and *gbeginH* and *gbeginV* are updated with the new ball location.

Facing the consequences

When the user leaves the constraining graphic (i.e. bumps into a wall) or lets go of the mouse — effectively putting the ball down — he must face the consequence of losing a life. Let's look briefly at the script that controls the subtraction of the life balls in the lower-right diamond. These five balls are all separate sprites residing in sprite channels 31 to 35.

The ball counter is updated with a custom handler called, appropriately, *counter* (Figure 9-f). The *counter* handler is called from the *idle* handler. The *idle* handler is another of Lingo's predefined event handlers. This handler executes every time Lingo has nothing else to do, hence its name, *idle*. The *idle* handler is the most frequently executed handler; consequently the *counter* handler is constantly being run, updating the ball count in the lower right-hand diamond.

The *counter* script uses an array of *if...then* statements to check what the count in the variable *gCount* is. It then turns the appropriate ball invisible. The movie starts with the *gCount* variable set to an initial value of 1. Remember, in line **P** of the *mouseDown* handler shown in Figure 9-c, the value in *gCount* was increased by 1. So, as the value in *gCount* goes up, one more ball disappears from the stage until all five balls are gone. At this point the game is over.

```
Movie Script 1:moviescript

moviesc    1    Internal

counter

on counter
  global gCount

  if gCount = 2 then
    set the visible of sprite 31 to FALSE
  end if

  if gCount = 3 then
    set the visible of sprite 32 to FALSE
  end if

  if gCount = 4 then
    set the visible of sprite 33 to FALSE
  end if

  if gCount = 5 then
    set the visible of sprite 34 to FALSE
  end if

  if gCount = 6 then
    set the visible of sprite 35 to FALSE
  end if

  updatestage
end counter
```

Figure 9-f. The *counter* script.

Going to the next level

Once the user reaches the last screen (Figure 9-4) he has the choice of quitting or going to the next level — the next location on the Internet which was chosen at random at the beginning of the game.

When the user clicks on the next-level button, it calls the script shown in Figure 9-5. Once again, several global variables are initialized **Ⓐ** before the script enters into an *if...then* statement. **Ⓑ** This *if...then* statement illustrates an excellent point about designing multimedia for the Web as we'll see here:

The purpose of the next-level button is simply to make a beep sound and send the user to the next URL (contained in the variable *gnextlevel* as discussed earlier) by using the Net-specific Lingo *gotoNetPage*. The reality of the Web, unfortunately, is that things don't always move as swiftly as you'd like them to. Invariably, there will be a delay from the time the user clicks the button and the time the page is retrieved from the Web. Meanwhile the user isn't sure whether the button has actually done anything and may grow impatient and click again (and possibly again and again). If not for the use of this *if...then* statement and the *gflag* variable, each mouse click would send out another *gotoNetPage* command, preempting the first.

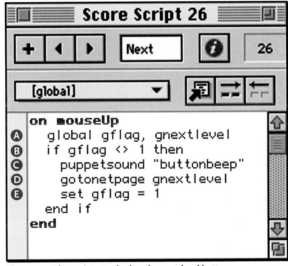

Figure 9-5. The script attached to the next level button.

Ironically, the impatient user who tries to make things go faster by frequent clicking may never get anywhere!

This problem has been neatly solved with this *if...then* statement. **Ⓑ** At the start of the movie the variable *gflag* has been set to 0. So the first time the user clicks on the next-level button, the statements after the *if...then* line are executed, since *gflag* does not equal 1. The first line of these commands **Ⓒ** plays a sound called *buttonbeep*. Next, the *gotoNetPage* command **Ⓓ** calls the URL contained in the variable *gnextlevel*. The last line of the script **Ⓔ** sets *gflag* to 1, causing any subsequent clicks to ignore the commands in the *if...then* statement.

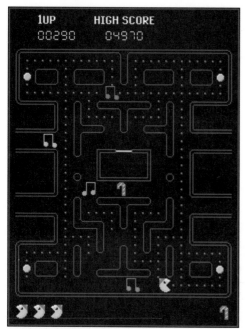

Figure 9-6. As the *Jazzman* game is played the user's score is continuously updated at the top of the screen.

Figure 9-7. The *Game Over* screen showing the current score and the high score.

There you have the basic workings of the maze. There are a few more tricks for you to discover as you explore the sample maze file provided on the CD. Use the sample file to create your own unique maze and join us on the World Wide Maze.

The personal touch

Net Lingo also lets you create a personalized experience in Shockwave. With the Net-specific Lingo *setPref* and *getPref,* you can retain specific information about individual users, such as the high score in a game or the user's name. Using this information on subsequent visits can be a valuable technique in personalizing your site. *SetPref* and *getPref* allow you to write a text file, containing whatever information you choose, to the user's hard drive and read this information back into the Shockwave movie when the user visits your site again. Because the prefs are written to the user's disk, the information is persistent days or even months later.

An excellent example of using preferences in Shockwave is demonstrated in a game called *Jazzman* from The Article 19 Group. *Jazzman* uses the *pref* commands to keep track of the individual's personal high score. As the user plays *Jazzman,* the score is continually updated (Figure 9-6). When the player uses up his last *Jazzman* life, the *Game Over* screen pops up (Figure 9-7), showing the current score and high score totals. This high score is recorded to the player's disk in a Shockwave preferences file.

Reading the high score

On the start of the movie, a custom handler called *checkmyprefs* is called (Figure 9-8). This handler first initializes a global variable called *gprefsfilename.* **Ⓐ** This variable has been set to the file name of the prefs file that the game will use. This file is called *a19_jazz.*

We'll see how the movie uses this variable in a moment. The next line **B** demonstrates an excellent tip for Shockwave authoring.

Author, author

Commands such as *setPref* and *getPref* are very difficult to test during authoring because Net-specific Lingo is understood only by the Shockwave plug-in and not by Director itself. However, the *runmode* Lingo command allows you to test whether the movie is in *author* mode (meaning, in Director) or not, and generate two separate results based on whether you are or not.

If the movie is not in *author* mode, the next line **C** uses *getPref* to set a variable called *mypref* to the text contained in the pref file *a19_jazz*. Remember, the variable *gprefsfilename* was set to equal *a19_jazz*. Next the handler uses the *voidP* Lingo command to test whether or not the variable *mypref* contains any text. **D** This checks to see if there is any text in *a19_jazz*. If it's empty (meaning this is the first time this user has played the game) the variable *mypref* is void. In this case, the *a19_jazz* file is written to the user's drive and given a default high score of 500

See it in action

A Shockwave version of *Jazzman* is located on the CD in *samples/ jazzman/*. To play the game, open the file, *jazzman.htm* in your Web browser.

Lingo tip

The *runmode* command can be used with any of Lingo's Net-specific commands to provide an alternative value if the movie is in *author* mode. This allows you to run your movies in Director without getting a script error.

If the movie is in Director, the *runmode* is *author*. If the *runmode* is not *author*, then the movie has been afterburned and is playing on the Web.

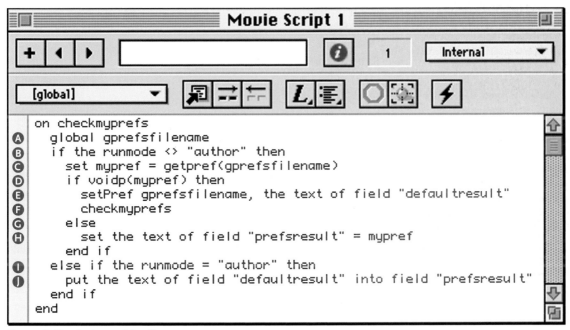

```
on checkmyprefs
  global gprefsfilename
  if the runmode <> "author" then
    set mypref = getpref(gprefsfilename)
    if voidp(mypref) then
      setPref gprefsfilename, the text of field "defaultresult"
      checkmyprefs
    else
      set the text of field "prefsresult" = mypref
    end if
  else if the runmode = "author" then
    put the text of field "defaultresult" into field "prefsresult"
  end if
end
```

Figure 9-8. The *checkmyprefs* handler.

```
                          Movie Script 1

+  ◀  ▶  [                              ]  ⓘ  [ 1 ]  [ Internal      ▼ ]

[global]              ▼   [icons]        L  ≣  O ⊡  ⚡

      on setmyprefs
 Ⓐ       global gprefsfilename
 Ⓑ       if the runmode <> "author" then
 Ⓒ         setPref gprefsfilename, the text of field "prefsresult"
         end if
      end
```

Figure 9-9. The *setmyprefs* handler.

The Article 19 Group

http://www.article19.com/

The Article 19 Group Inc. specializes in the research, design, production, and implementation of New Media and Knowledge Technology products and systems. Their core competencies combine knowledge engineering and interactive multimedia production that enable them to offer their clients a complete solution to communication objectives. The Article 19 Group provides services and products for a variety of markets including: corporate training, performance support, education, edutainment, organizational communications, marketing, and technical support. For more information, see their Web site.

points. Ⓔ The text field called *defaultresult* contains this default score. The handler then starts over, by calling itself. Ⓕ This ensures that *mypref* will not be void the next time through the handler and will jump to the *else* line of the *if...then* statement. Ⓖ The next line Ⓗ sets the text of the field called *prefsresult* to the text contained in *mypref*. This is the field on the stage that displays the high score to the user.

If the movie is in the *author* mode (line Ⓘ), the field *prefsresult* is set to the default high score contained in the field *defaultresult*. Ⓙ

Saving the high score

When the game reaches the Game Over frame, another custom handler called *setmyprefs* is set into action (Figure 9-9). The first line of this script Ⓐ calls the global variable that contained the name of the pref file *(a19_jazz)*. Next the *runmode* command is used again Ⓑ to make sure the game is not in *author* mode. If not in *author* mode, the handler uses the *setPref* Lingo command to set the file *a19_jazz (gprefsfilename)* to the text in the field *prefsresult*. Ⓒ This field has been updated with the high score during the course of game play.

As you can see, this one simple example shows the potential and power to maximize the user's experience by writing out personal preferences to the hard drive of each individual that comes to your site.

In the next chapter we'll talk about more ways you can maximize the user's experience when they visit your site.

Shockwave Studio

10

Maximizing the User's Experience

One of the problems with Shockwave — indeed, with any technology above and beyond basic HTML — is that not all of your audience will have the plug-in installed. Even if most of them go and get the plug-in, there will always be some people who use systems not supported by Shockwave (there is currently no support for any UNIX system and there may never be), who are unable to get the plug-in to install correctly, or who are just unwilling to install it. Thus most sites will want to offer a "normal" version of the site, as well as a shocked version.

In this chapter we'll look at ways of solving these problems, as well as some of the little things you can use to finish off your shocked pages and maximize the user's experience.

Warning: Shockwave required

Since they know that some users won't have Shockwave, many sites just put up an entry page that describes the requirements for the site and tells users where to get what they need before moving into the main site. This is an area of Web site design that is largely ignored. Instead of designing these pages into the total experience of the site, too often the page is very bland with a link to the main site and the standard orange "Get Shockwave" button (seen at left).

Fly Qaswa Air

Qaswa Air, Ammon Haggerty's repository of creative works, uses an airport metaphor to navigate you through the site. The first screen visitors see is the airport hub, offering a choice of standard (non-Shockwave) or Shockwave (Figure 10-1) pages. Clicking on the Shockwave hub takes you to a message from the

Many of the problems discussed here have to do with the Netscape plug-in architecture, which requires users to download the Shockwave plug-in, install it, quit and restart Netscape, and re-enter the URL. Microsoft's ActiveX technology simplifies this process by asking if the user wants to download the Shockwave ActiveX Control and then simply doing it. At this point ActiveX is not available for all platforms.

As mentioned in Chapter 1, Macromedia has made deals to include Shockwave with both Netscape's and Microsoft's browsers, so at some point in the future Shockwave will be widely deployed.

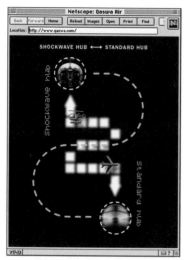

Figure 10-1. When visitors arrive at Ammon Haggerty's site at *http://www.qaswa.com/* they are first presented with a choice of standard or Shockwave hubs.

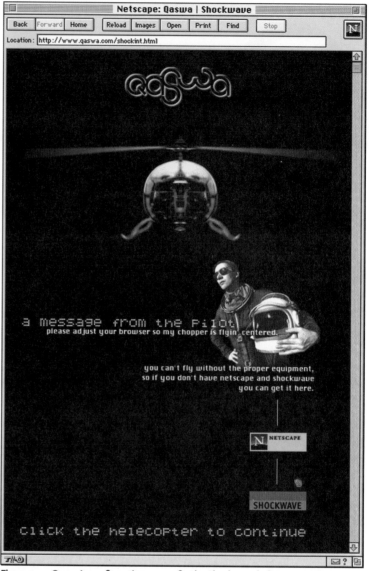

Figure 10-2. Qaswa's configuration screen for the Shockwave hub.

pilot asking you to "adjust your browser so my chopper is flyin' centered" (Figure 10-2). He also tells you that "you can't fly without the proper equipment" and points the visitor to the Shockwave download site. Once properly equipped, the visitor enters the site by clicking on the helicopter. Qaswa's beautiful Shockwave interface (Figure 10-3) offers navigational choices

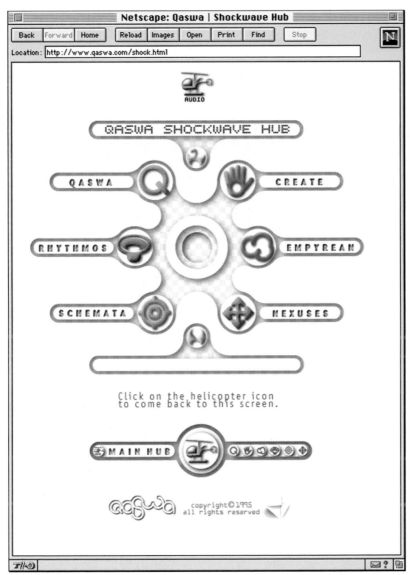

Figure 10-3. Qaswa's Shockwave interface.

and information about each section. Because it's designed with such an interesting shape and with a white stage on a white Web page, it makes it impossible to tell where the Shockwave ends and the HTML starts. This creates a much more immersive experience, making users almost totally unaware Shockwave is even being used.

Template for META refresh

```
<HTML>
<HEAD>
<TITLE>Title this page</TITLE>
<META http-equiv="refresh" content="15; URL=http://webreview.com/nonshocked/">
</HEAD>
<BODY>
<EMBED HEIGHT=300 WIDTH=300 SRC="http://webreview.com/shockwave.dcr">
</BODY>
</HTML>
```

Figure 10-4. This page contains a Shockwave movie that sends the user to the shocked version of the site. Users without Shockwave will be redirected to a non-shocked page after 15 seconds.

Testing for Shockwave

Another way to solve the problem of whether or not the user has Shockwave installed is to use a Shockwave test page. Basically, this consists of an opening page with a small Shockwave file embedded in it. This file is a loader movie (we'll discuss loader movies later in this chapter), which sends the Shockwave-equipped visitor to the shocked section of the site. Users without Shockwave stay put. You can provide a link for visitors to go to the non-shocked section, or use a *META* tag to send them there. Figure 10-4 shows sample HTML for using the *META refresh* tag. In this example, after 15 seconds the user's browser connects to *http://webreview.com/nonshocked.* Change the time delay by changing the number before the semicolon; change the URL by changing the text after *URL=*. Note that this *META refresh* tag must be in the head of the document, as in this template. This a very simple method to automatically move users from one page to another.

Testing for Shockwave using Javascript

Another way to test for the presence of the Shockwave plug-in is by using Javascript. Figure 10-5 shows a sample HTML page for this use of Javascript. In this example, the script tests to see if the visitor is using Netscape 3.0 or greater and that the Shockwave for Director MIME-type (application/x-director) is present. If so, the script uses the *document.write* command to write the *EMBED* tag to the page. If the visitor's browser is something other than

Template for testing for the Shockwave plug-in using Javascript

```
<HTML>
<HEAD>
<TITLE>Title this page</TITLE>
</HEAD>
<BODY>
 <script language="javascript">
 <!--
 if (parseInt(navigator.appVersion) >= 3 &&
 navigator.mimeTypes["application/x-director"]) {
 document.write("<EMBED SRC='shockwave.dcr' HEIGHT=320 WIDTH=240>");
 } else if (parseInt(navigator.appVersion) < 3) {
 document.write('<OBJECT CLASSID="clsid:166B1BCA-3F9C-11CF-8075-444553540000"');
 document.write('CODEBASE="http://active.macromedia.com/director/cabs/sw.cab#version=5,0,1,61"');
 document.write('WIDTH="300" HEIGHT="300" NAME="Shockwave"');
 document.write('ID="swmovie1">');
 document.write('<PARAM NAME="SRC" VALUE="jazzman.dcr">');
 document.write('<PARAM NAME="BGCOLOR" VALUE="#000000">');
 document.write('<PARAM NAME="PALETTE" VALUE="foreground">');
 document.write('<embed SRC=shockwave.dcr height=300 width=300 PALETTE=foreground');
 document.write('BGCOLOR=#000000 PLUGINSPAGE=http://www.macromedia.com/shockwave/>');
 document.write('</OBJECT>');
 } else {
 document.write("You don't have the shockwave plug-in!");
 }
 // -->
 </script>
 </BODY>
 </HTML>
```

Figure 10-5. This script was contributed by Nick Heinle, author of the next book in this series, *Web Scripting Studio: Designing with JavaScript*. Look for it this summer from O'Reilly & Associates.

Netscape 3.0, the *OBJECT* tag is written to the page. This will allow users with Microsoft Internet Explorer and the ActiveX Control to see the Shockwave. If the Shockwave plug-in is not present, an alternate message is written to the page.

Unfortunately, at this time, Microsoft Internet Explorer for the Macintosh does not support Javascript, so this method will not work for those users.

For more on the *EMBED* and *OBJECT* tags and adding Shockwave movies to HTML pages, see Appendix A.

Integrating Shockwave into the page

It's interesting that while Web design has moved away from the blocky designs of the early Web (a square banner plunked on the top of the page with edge-to-edge text below it) — and towards more sophisticated designs using tables, frames, transparent

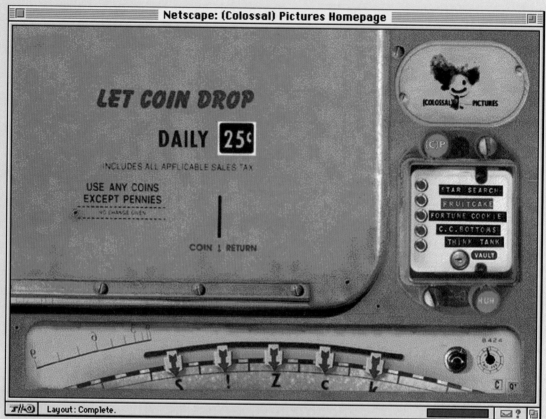

Colossal Pictures, *http://www.colossal.com/*.

Can you spot the Shockwave on these pages?

The Web developer's fondest fantasy is to have enough bandwidth to deliver a rich, CD-quality multimedia experience, not on a silver platter, but over the Internet. When I first saw Zoloft — Spectacle Entertainment's weekly episodic vision of a futuristic society — I was immediately struck by the fact that a CD-quality experience was being delivered within the constraints of online technology. With skilled use of compression techniques (what Josh Feldman, Zoloft's designer, describes as "overly JPEGed JPEGs") and careful use of available resources and technologies such as Shockwave, Zoloft's creators deliver a media-rich environment using very little bandwidth. "Our goal," says Josh, "is that the person with a 14.4K modem would be able to enjoy Zoloft without dying!"

Colossal Pictures' site offers visitors a similar low-bandwidth, highly graphical experience. Though not an ongoing series like Zoloft, Colossal's site gives visitors "a sense of the creative confusion, accumulation, and managed chaos" that characterizes their work.

Zoloft, *http://www.spectacle.com/zoloft/*.

Having a hard time finding the Shockwave on these pages? It's because it is so well integrated into the design. Both Colossal (left) and Zoloft (right) use Shockwave as navigational tools (outlined in red). Zoloft also uses a very small Shockwave movie (lower right) to deliver voice-over narration.

Figure 10-7. Colossal Pictures' home page is divided into five frames (outlined in red). There is one area for content, two navigational areas, and two Javascript helper frames that are hidden when the window is set to the correct height and width. Here the window has been enlarged to show the two helper frames (with black backgrounds).

GIFs, background tiles, and such — many Shockwave designers limit themselves to the square-cut shape of the Director stage.

Most Shockwave content consists of a rectangular or square movie plunked onto a page with no regard for what's going on around it. While there are many instances where this is perfectly acceptable, integrating the Shockwave movie onto the page — even if it is as simple as matching the color of the stage with the background color of the Web page — can increase the user's enjoyment of your site. The sites shown on the previous pages are excellent examples of integrating Shockwave into the total look of the page.

Template for opening new window using Javascript

```
<HTML>
<HEAD>
<TITLE>
Title this page
</TITLE>
<script language=javascript>
</script>
</HEAD>
<BODY onLoad = 'myWin = window.open("test.html","myWin","directories=0,toolbar=0,
location=0,status=0,menubar=0,resizable=no,scrollbars=no,height=300,width=300")'>
</BODY>
</HTML>
```

Figure 10-8. Upon loading this page, a new window will open. Be sure not to insert any carriage returns in the *BODY* string.

Targeting frames and controlling windows

Another very effective way to achieve a dynamic user experience is by using Shockwave in conjunction with frames. Colossal Pictures' Web site takes this concept one step further. Using Shockwave frames and Javascript allows Colossal to better control the interface to their site by automatically opening a new window to a specific height and width and without the button bars and location field of the standard browser window.

Within the main interface Colossal uses two Shockwave movies as navigational elements. When a button is clicked by the user, another window is opened up with the new page in it. The trick here is that they are using Javascript to create the new window, although Javascript does not as yet work in Lingo.

So how do they do it? John Belew, lead programmer for Colossal, shared the trick with me. On the main page are two hidden frames (Figure 10-7), which John calls "Javascript helper frames." When a *gotoNetPage* command is issued from the Shockwave navigational movies, the HTML is targeted into one of these hidden frames. Within the HTML is the Javascript to create the new window. As John explains it, they use *gotoNetPage* calls from the Shockwave movie and target these Javascript helper frames, and then the window creation is handled by the Javascript *onload* event. The document loads into the helper

Loading Fortune Cookie
About 312k...

Loading Fortune Cookie
About 312k...

Loading Fortune Cookie
About 312k...

Loading Fortune Cookie
About 312k...

Loading Fortune Cookie
About 312k...

Colossal Pictures' loader movie (above), illustrated by Dave Freemont, entertains the visitor with a short animation while telling them the real Shockwave is on its way. Being a traditional artist, Dave wasn't entirely clear on just what John Belew wanted when he asked him to create the animation. As John tells it, "I actually told the artist I wanted 'loading' and he misheard me as 'load in' and it turned out just perfectly. So that's his concept of 'load in,' not knowing what that meant."

frame, and all the variables for intermovie and interwindow communication pass between Shockwave, Javascript, and CGI.

To target the Javascript helper frame from a Shockwave movie, a *gotoNetPage* command is issued in a *mouseUp* handler as shown here:

```
on mouseUp
    gotoNetPage "URL_for_the_page", "target_frame_name"
end mouseUp
```

Figure 10-8 shows a basic Javascript template for creating a new window. The *onload* event handler in the *BODY* tag is triggered when the page is loaded into the browser window. This *onload* handler opens a new window called *"myWin"* at the height and width specified, and loads the file *"test.html"* into the window. In addition, the directory buttons, tool bar, location window, status bar, menu bar, and scroll bars are turned off and the window is made non-resizable.

The loader movie

If you've ever waited for a large Shockwave movie to download, you know that chasing the Macromedia logo around with the mouse gets real old, real fast. One way you can keep the user from losing interest while your Shockwave movie downloads is through the use of a loader movie. A loader movie is a very small movie that occupies the user with a short game or animation while the real movie downloads. Let's look at how a simple loader movie is put together.

Loading Fortune Cookie About 312k....   Loading Fortune Cookie About 312k....   Loading Fortune Cookie About 312k....   Loading Fortune Cookie About 312k....   Loading Fortune Cookie About 312k....

In a movie script, create a *startMovie* handler, which calls your real Shockwave movie using a *gotoNetMovie* command (Figure 10-9). As this loader movie begins to play, it immediately calls the movie specified at the URL in the *gotoNetMovie* command. The user can then interact with your loader movie, while the real movie loads in the background. Once the movie is loaded, it replaces the loader movie on the page and begins to play.

When creating a loader movie, there are several tips to keep in mind. The loader movie should be the exact same pixel dimensions as the real movie. If the real movie is larger than the loader movie, the real movie will be cropped to the width and height specified in the *EMBED* tag. Also, the palette for the loader movie should be the same as the real movie to avoid palette conflicts on 8-bit systems when going from one movie to the next.

Figure 10-9. The loader movie script.

The dreaded -108 error

One big frustration for users viewing Shockwave on the Macintosh has been the -108 out of memory error. Apparently caused by a fault in the Netscape plug-in API that causes Shockwave files to be held in memory and not fully released, even when the movie has been closed, this error can only be remedied by quitting the browser and restarting. Doubly frustrating for the user is that the error doesn't show up until

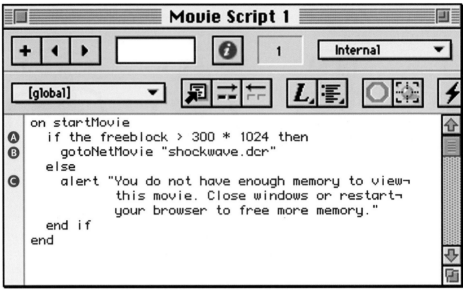

```
    Movie Script 1
    +  ◄  ►  ▢        ⓘ      1      Internal ▼

    [global] ▼    ⊡ ⇄ ⇤    L,⋮    ◯ ⊡    ⚡

     on startMovie
 Ⓐ     if the freeblock > 300 * 1024 then
 Ⓑ       gotoNetMovie "shockwave.dcr"
       else
 Ⓒ       alert "You do not have enough memory to view¬
                this movie. Close windows or restart¬
                your browser to free more memory."
       end if
     end
```

Figure 10-10. The loader movie script with the memory check.

after the Shockwave movie has been downloaded. There are few things worse than sitting through a large download only to be told at the end that there isn't enough memory to play the Shockwave movie! Although this problem can't be remedied, you can help Mac users out a bit by running a test to see if they have a large enough free block of RAM (Figure 10-10) to run the movie. If they do, send them to the movie; if not, give them an alert.

The script first checks to see if there is a free, contiguous block of RAM large enough for the movie to load into. Ⓐ The *freeBlock* command measures the amount in bytes, so the 300 figure in this script should be changed to the size in kilobytes of your movie. If there is a free block of memory large enough to accommodate the movie, then the *gotoNetMovie* command is issued. Ⓑ If not, an alert box pops up telling the user what they must do. Ⓒ

Using this simple script can go a long way towards saving your vistors from the headache of waiting through a large download, just to find out they can't view the file.

In the next chapter we'll talk about the final and possibly the most important factor in maximizing the user experience — audio.

11

Audio Compression with Shockwave

Free audio Xtras from Macromedia
The Shockwave Audio Xtra WAV file converter for Director for Windows 95/NT and the SoundEdit Streaming Audio Toolkit for Power Macintosh are available from the Macromedia Web site at: *http://www.macromedia.com/ shockwave/devtools.html.*

Note: The Shockwave Audio compression Xtras for internal Director sounds are included in each of the Afterburner for Director packages.

The first time I saw Shockwave I was immediately struck, not by the fact that an interactive Director movie was playing on a Web page, but that there was music and sound playing on the page.

Back then, sound on the Web was always very intrusive — not at all a seamless part of the user experience. You had to click on a link to a sound file, which would then download; a helper application would then open — taking you away from the Web page — and play the sound. Of course there are now dozens of ways to add sound seamlessly to a Web page — but at the time of Shockwave's release the fact that you could get sound so transparently through a Web page reinforced to me just how effective sound can be in enhancing the experience of the user.

Of course all this wonderful sound came at a high cost: Shockwave's AfterBurner offered no compression for audio. Thus adding an audio file to a Shockwave movie increased the size of the movie by the file size of the audio. And, as you may know, even the simplest of sounds can produce very large file sizes. That all changed in July 1996 with the release of Shockwave Audio.

Now, not only can internal Director sounds be compressed as much as 176:1 using the Shockwave Audio compression Xtra, but audio files can be streamed over the Internet.

Compressing sounds with Afterburner

With the Shockwave Audio Xtras available free from Macromedia's Web site, you can compress sounds imported into the cast of a Director movie.

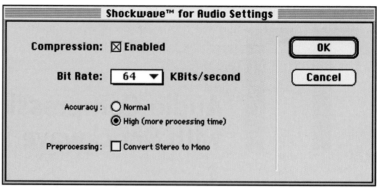

Figure 11-1. The *Shockwave for Audio Settings* dialog box.

Shockwave sells tools

When Shockwave Audio was introduced, Windows users were dismayed to learn that there was no way to create streaming Shockwave Audio files on a PC. The popular consensus among Mac users was that it was Macromedia's way of making up to them for their lack of a Mac plug-in at the initial release of Shockwave for Director in 1995. Actually, the reason was much simpler than that. Marcos Sanchez, former product manager for Shockwave put it plainly, "Shockwave drives tool sales." Macromedia has no sound tool for Windows, hence no streaming audio development on Windows. Soon after the initial release of Shockwave Audio, Macromedia released an Xtra for Director for Windows that allows users to create streaming audio files from within the application. Sounds like it would be a great thing for Mac users as well, but don't hold your breath; Macromedia still sells Sound Edit 16, a sound editing application.

To enable audio compression in Director, select *Xtras/Shockwave for Audio Settings* in Director (Figure 11-1). Enable audio compression by selecting the check box. Next select a bit rate from the popup menu. The lower the number, the better the compression and poorer the sound quality. Next, select an accuracy setting. Choosing *Convert Stereo to Mono* will further reduce file size and quality.

Although Shockwave compression is very good, using internal sound should be reserved for small sound clips. This is because

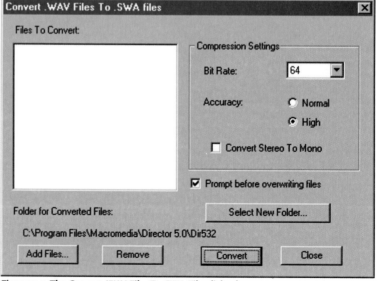

Figure 11-2. The *Convert .WAV Files To .SWA Files* dialog box.

internal sounds are embedded within the shocked movie, which must be fully downloaded to begin playing. Large audio files, such as songs or long narratives, can be compressed and streamed over the Internet using your Director movie as a player.

Creating streaming audio files in Windows

Windows users can convert WAV files to streaming audio files (SWA) right in Director. Select **Xtras/Convert WAV to SWA**. This brings up the dialog box shown in Figure 11-2. Next, click on the *Add Files* button to bring up an *Open File* dialog box, where you can select the files you want to convert. Then select a bit rate and accuracy setting and click *Convert*.

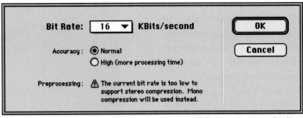

Figure 11-3. The *Shockwave for Audio Settings* dialog box in Sound Edit 16, seen here, is nearly identical to the one in Director (Figure 11-1).

Creating streaming audio files on a Macintosh

To create streaming audio files on a Macintosh, you must use Sound Edit 16 from Macromedia. To create an SWA file in Sound Edit, open your sound clip and select **Xtras/Shockwave for Audio Settings**.This brings up a dialog box nearly identical to the one in Director (Figure 11-3). Select the desired bit rate and accuracy settings and click *OK*. Next, select **File/Export**, which brings up the *Export* dialog box seen in Figure 11-4. Name your file and select *SWA File* from the *Export Type* popup menu.

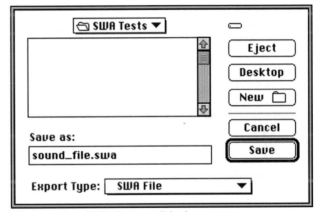

Figure 11-4. Sound Edit 16's *Export* dialog box.

Once you've created your streaming audio files, you can upload them to your Web server and play them from your Shockwave movie. Let's take a look at our next example to see how this is done.

Listen, it's *OddoRadio*

Tommy Oddo, a Texas-based Web designer, created an interesting audio player in Director as part of a self-promotional Shockwave movie called *OddoRadio*. When you first arrive at *OddoRadio*,

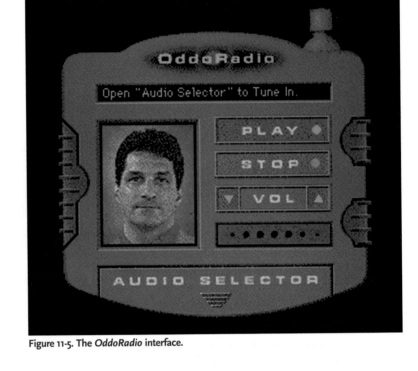

Figure 11-5. The *OddoRadio* interface.

Oddo Design

http://www.oddo.com/

Tommy Oddo began his career as a graphic designer over 17 years ago. After attending the Art Institute of Atlanta, he relocated to Houston where he runs his Web design and marketing business. His work has garnered many design and illustration awards and has been featured in several books. You can find out more about Tommy by tuning in to his Web site.

Figure 11-6. *OddoRadio* with the Audio Selector drawer open.

you're presented with a fun, techy looking interface reminiscent of something you might get as a Happy Meal toy from McDonald's (Figure 11-5). Click on the *Audio Selector,* and a drawer full of audio selections pops open (Figure 11-6). Clicking on one of the selections causes the drawer to snap shut and the first portion of the audio to preload as a buffer. Once the buffer is preloaded, you can click the *Play* button to start the audio stream.

Let's take a look inside *OddoRadio* to see how streaming audio works.

First, in order to use streaming audio files with your Director movie, an *SWA file Xtra cast member reference* must be placed in the cast of the movie. Select **Insert/Other/SWA Streaming Xtra.** This reference file appears as cast member 4 in the *OddoRadio* movie (Figure 11-7) and will be used later to specify the URL of the streaming audio file.

When the user makes a selection from the *Audio Selector* drawer, it calls a *mouseUp* script attached to the graphic. This script simply calls a custom handler for the particular audio

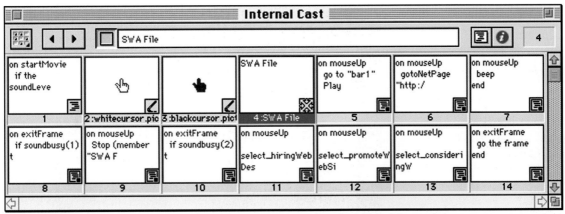

Figure 11-7. The SWA file Xtra cast member reference appears as cast member 4 in *OddoRadio's* cast window.

selection. In this example, we'll look at the script for the *About OddoRadio* button, which looks like this:

```
on mouseUp
    select_aboutOdRadio
end
```

This script has just one purpose: to call the *select_about OdRadio* handler seen in Figure 11-8.

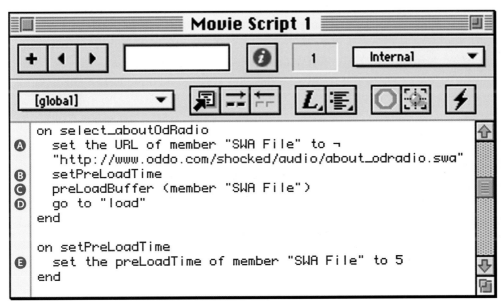

Figure 11-8. The *select_aboutOdRadio* handler.

The first line of the *select_aboutOdRadio* handler sets the URL of the cast member called *SWA File* to the URL of the

Figure 11-9. The *OddoRadio* status window during the *load* frames.

about_odradio.swa file. **A** This cast member is the SWA file Xtra reference that was inserted into the cast earlier. Next, the script calls another handler **B** named *setPreLoadTime*.

This handler, also shown in Figure 11-8, **E** simply sets the preload time of the SWA file to 5 seconds. That is, the file will download for 5 seconds before starting to play. After setting the preload time, the handler ends and the *select_aboutOdRadio* handler resumes. The next line in this handler **C** uses the *preLoadBuffer* command to start the download of the specified portion of the SWA file into memory. Lastly, the handler sends the movie to the frame called *load*. **D**

This frame starts a four-frame series that animates the ellipsis at the end of the words "Thank You. Selection Now Loading..." in *OddoRadio's* status window (Figure 11-9). This gives

OddoRadio compression

Shockwave Audio compression can produce some fairly astounding results, as evidenced by the files in Tommy's OddoRadio. Tommy recorded all his sounds at 16 bits/44.100 kHz and downsampled them to 16/22.050. After equalizing and normalizing the tracks in Sound Edit 16, Tommy exported the sounds as SWA files at a bit rate of 16 K/Bits per second achieving the amazing results below:

File name	Original size	SWA size
about_odradio.swa	3.0MB	141K
hire_firm.swa	7.0MB	326K
promote_web.swa	4.7MB	223K
want_site.swa	4.2MB	197K
web_cost.swa	4.8MB	227K
where_begin.swa	4.2MB	197K

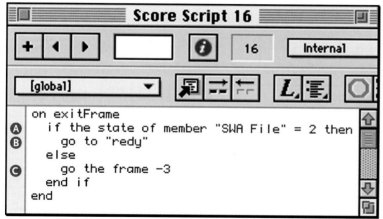

```
Score Script 16

+  ◀  ▶  [      ]  (i)  16   Internal

[global]           ▼  🔲 ⇄ ⊢ L 🗐 O

   on exitFrame
A    if the state of member "SWA File" = 2 then
B      go to "redy"
     else
C      go the frame -3
     end if
   end
```

Figure 11-10. The *load* frames' *exitFrame* handler.

the user a clue that something is happening in the background,
and that the movie isn't simply frozen. The last of the frames in
this series calls the *exitFrame* handler seen in Figure 11-10 when
the movie exits the frame.

This script uses an *if...then* statement **A** to check if the state
of the SWA file is 2. The Lingo *the state of member* checks the
"state" of an SWA file and returns a numerical code
depending on the state. The number 2 means that
preloading is finished. (For a list of possible states and
their numeric codes, see Appendix B.) If the preload is
done, the movie goes to the frame called *redy*. **B** If
preloading is not done, the movie jumps back 3 frames **C**
— back to the start of the ellipsis animation.

Once preloading is finished and the movie has
moved to the *redy* frame, it now waits for the user to
press the *Play* button, while the words "Selection Ready.
Please Press Play" blink in the status window (Figure
11-11). Tommy adds another nice visual touch at this
point by raising the antenna on the radio.

When the user presses *Play*, the script in Figure
11-12 is activated. This script sends the movie to the
frame called *bar1* **A** and plays the SWA file. **B**

The *bar1* frame starts a series of frames that, like the *load*
frames, animate the ellipsis at the end of the words "Thank You.

Why buffer?

When audio is streamed over the
Internet, it is necessary to send a
certain amount of audio data to the
user's computer memory before
play begins. This preloaded data is
called a buffer. In order to ensure an
uninterrupted stream of audio, the
player plays the data from this
buffered memory, allowing more
data to download while it is being
played. The higher the buffer is set,
the better chance you will have of
uninterrupted audio, however, the
higher the buffer, the longer the
user will have to wait before
playback begins.

Figure 11-11. Waiting for the user to press "Play."
Note the antenna is now raised.

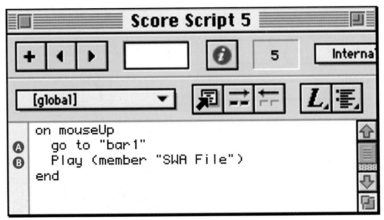

Figure 11-12. The *Play* button script.

Selection Now Playing...." As the movie passes through each of the frames in this series, the *exitFrame* handler shown in Figure 11-13 is called. This handler checks to see if the SWA file has finished playing. An *if...then* statement Ⓐ checks the state of the SWA file. A state of *5* means the file is done playing. Then a *Stop* command is issued Ⓑ and the movie goes to the frame called *strtc,* the *Audio Selector* frame. If the file is not done playing, the movie jumps back to the beginning of the ellipsis animation. Ⓒ

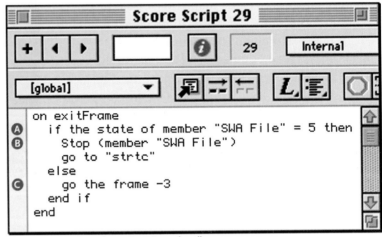

Figure 11-13. The *bar 1* frames' *exitFrame* handler.

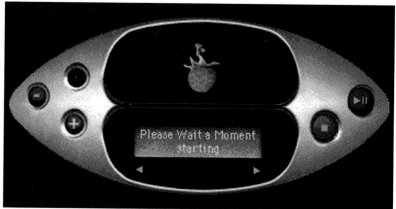

Figure 11-14. Raspberry Media's Shockwave Audio player.

Using external parameters

In the example above, the URLs for the SWA files are hard-coded in the Shockwave file. While this is a perfectly fine method, it has several drawbacks. If you want to change the selections in the file, or if you move the SWA files to another location on your server, the original movie must be edited, reburned, and uploaded. Also, if you wanted to use the same player on different pages, with different audio selections, a new movie for each page would have to be created by you, and downloaded by the user.

Using Lingo, Shockwave movies can access parameters that are included in the *EMBED* or *OBJECT* tags of an HTML document. By changing these external parameters, you can easily alter the functionality of your movies, including URL links and preload times for SWA files, as we'll see in our next example.

Raspberry Media has created a Shockwave audio player to showcase some of the examples of their professional sound design services (Figure 11-14). The Lingo for the Raspberry player, written by Josh Kopel of Articus Media Labs, uses external parameters to transfer the base URL for a group of SWA files, the list of SWA file names, the preload time for the files, and a list of text names for each of the songs into the Shockwave movie.

The player's external parameters are located in the *EMBED* tag of the HTML page (Figure 11-15). The parameters are read

See it in action
The Raspberry Shockwave player is located on the CD in *source/raspbery.dir*.

```
<HTML>
<HEAD>
<TITLE>Sound Effects</TITLE>
</HEAD>
<BODY BGCOLOR="#000000">

<EMBED width=416 height=171 SRC="rasp_player.dcr"
swURL="http://www.raspberrymedia.com/audio/"
swList="sound_eff.swa,blues.swa,reggae.swa"
swTEXT="Sound effects Medley,Blues Medley,Reggae Medley"
swPreLoadTime=4
animate = "YES">

</BODY>
</HTML>
```

Figure 11-15. The HTML for Raspberry Media's player contains several external parameters in the *EMBED* tag.

Raspberry Media

http://www.raspberrymedia.com/

Based in Sebastopol, CA, Raspberry Media is a design studio specializing in Web site development, graphic design, digital audio, and photography.

Over the past few years they have completed projects for an international clientele including Virgin Interactive, *Rolling Stone*, *GQ*, EMI Records, Mindscape, and the University of California.

Articus Media Labs

http://www.dev-com.com/~amlab/

Joshua A. Kopel is one of the directors of Articus Media Labs, Inc. a Web and multimedia development firm located in Philadelphia, PA.

into the Shockwave movie using the *if...then* statements shown in Figure 11-16. The first of these statements Ⓐ checks to see if there is an external parameter named *swText* in the *EMBED* tag, using the Lingo command *externalParamName.* If there is a parameter named *swText,* the string of text contained between the quotes in the *EMBED* tag is put into a variable named *myNameList* using the Lingo *externalParamValue.* Ⓑ If there isn't an *swText* parameter in the EMBED tag, a handler called *doerror* is executed Ⓒ and the process of reading in the parameters is aborted. Ⓓ

The *doerror* handler

The *doerror* handler (Figure 11-17), uses a *case* statement to display a dialog box to alert the user of the error. When the *doerror* handler is called from the *if...then* statement, a value of *1* is passed along to the *doerror* script. This value will tell the *doerror* script which error to display.

In the first line of the *doerror* script a variable called *what* is created to capture the value being passed from the *if...then* statement. Ⓐ This variable is then used in the *case* statement Ⓑ to determine which of the instances in the *case* statement to execute. In this instance, *what* has a value of 1, so the first line in the case statement is executed. Ⓒ This line Ⓓ brings up an alert box with the sentence, "Cannot find the list of song names." The

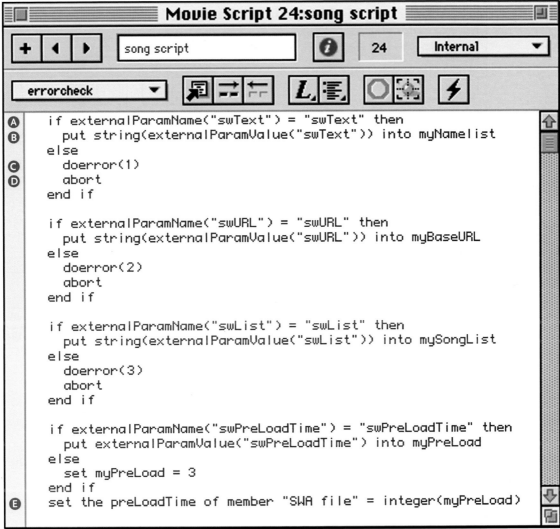

Figure 11-16. The Raspberry Media player uses *if...then* statements to capture the external parameters into variables.

doerror script then aborts. **E** The *abort* command causes the script to exit the *doerror* handler, without executing any further commands.

Capturing the remaining parameters

If there is no error in the first *if...then* statement of Figure 11-16, the rest of the statements are executed, capturing the remaining parameter values from the *EMBED* tag into separate variables.

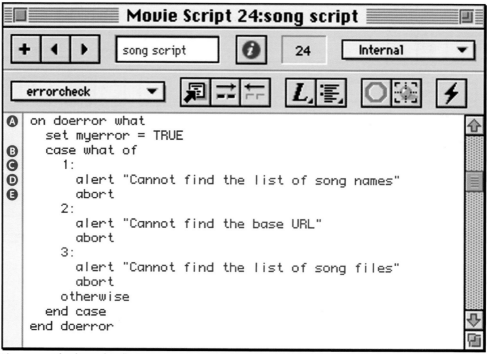

```
                Movie Script 24:song script

  +  ◀  ▶      song script      ⓘ    24    Internal   ▼

  errorcheck       ▼    🔲 ⇶ ⇷   L ≣   ◯ ⊡   ⚡

Ⓐ  on doerror what                                              ⇧
     set myerror = TRUE
Ⓑ   case what of
Ⓒ     1:
Ⓓ       alert "Cannot find the list of song names"
Ⓔ       abort
       2:
         alert "Cannot find the base URL"
         abort
       3:
         alert "Cannot find the list of song files"
         abort
       otherwise
     end case                                                  ⇩
  end doerror                                                  ▣
```

Figure 11-17. The *doerror* handler.

Once the parameters have been captured into the variables, they can be used to set preload times and the URLs of the songs, much as they were in *OddoRadio.* An example of this is seen in the final line of code shown in Figure 11-16. This line Ⓔ sets the *preLoadTime* of the SWA file to the integer contained in the variable called *myPreLoad.*

This is an excellent example of how you can customize Shockwave movies simply by altering external parameters in the HTML document.

Before Shockwave audio compression became available, designers were justified in ignoring this very important aspect of the overall user experience. Now, with the amazing amount of compression obtainable with Shockwave Audio, as well as the ability to stream, it is no longer necessary to neglect sound as you plan your next Shockwave project.

Serving Your Shockwave to the Masses

After you've authored your movie in Director, there are still a few more simple steps to making your Shockwave available for the world to see.

Step one: Afterburning

Although the Shockwave plug-in can display Director source files (files with a .dir extension), you will definitely want to "burn" your movie with Macromedia's free Afterburner utility. Afterburner comes as an Xtra (Macromedia's term for a plug-in) which, once installed, is available from Director's **Xtras** menu. Afterburning a Director file is as simple as selecting **Xtras/Afterburner** and saving the movie. Before burning your movie, be sure to remove any unused cast members such as graphics, sounds, and scripts. If cast members are removed, you should select **File/Save and Compact;** this will further reduce the size of your movies. Also, if you are using sounds in your movie, be sure to enable the Shockwave Audio compression following the instructions in Chapter 11.

Once your movie is burned, it can then be added to your HTML page using the *EMBED* or *OBJECT* tags.

Step two: HTML

To incorporate your Shockwave movie into your HTML page there are two tags you can use, *EMBED* and *OBJECT. EMBED* works with Netscape Navigator and other browsers compatible with the Netscape plug-in architecture, as well as Microsoft Internet Explorer. The *OBJECT* tag works with Microsoft Internet Explorer and provides a way for the Shockwave ActiveX Control to be

Template for embedding Shockwave in HTML

```
<HTML>
<HEAD>
<TITLE>
Title this page
</TITLE>
</HEAD>
<BODY>
<EMBED SRC="http://webreview.com/shockwave.dcr" HEIGHT=300 WIDTH=300
PALETTE="foreground" BGCOLOR="#000000"
PLUGINSPAGE="http://www.macromedia.com/shockwave">
</BODY>
</HTML>
```

Figure A-1.

downloaded automatically to the user if they don't already have it installed. Unfortunately, many other browsers, including Netscape, don't recognize the *OBJECT* tag.

The *EMBED* tag

Figure A-1 shows a template HTML page using the *EMBED* tag. You'll notice the *EMBED* tag includes attributes for *SRC, HEIGHT, WIDTH, PALETTE,* and *BGCOLOR.* Just as with the *IMG* tag, *SRC* indicates the URL of the Shockwave movie. This can be either an absolute or relative path. Although *HEIGHT* and *WIDTH* are optional for the *IMG* tag, they are critical for the *EMBED* tag. The *HEIGHT* and *WIDTH* attributes will crop the Shockwave movie to the size indicated. Without the *HEIGHT* and *WIDTH* specified, the movie is cropped to zero, making it not visible on the page. Also, if a *HEIGHT* or *WIDTH* is indicated that is larger than the stage size of the movie, any graphics located off the stage will appear on the Web page.

The *PALETTE* attribute lets you set whether the browser will use the movie's palette (foreground) or the browser's palette (background). The default, if the *PALETTE* attribute is not used, is background. The *BGCOLOR* attribute lets you set a hexadecimal color for the Shockwave movie space seen as the movie downloads. See Chapter 8 for more information on palettes and *BGCOLOR.*

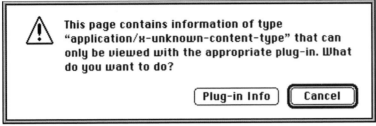

This page contains information of type "application/x-unknown-content-type" that can only be viewed with the appropriate plug-in. What do you want to do?

[Plug-in Info] [Cancel]

Figure A-2. The plug-in alert box.

Finally, the *PLUGINSPAGE* attribute provides a URL for users who don't have the Shockwave plug-in installed. This URL is used by Netscape to send the user to the correct page to get the plug-in when the *Plug-in Info* button is clicked in the alert box (Figure A-2).

Other external parameters may also be placed in the *EMBED* tag for use in the Shockwave movie. See Chapter 11 for more on using external parameters.

The *OBJECT* tag

If a user is browsing with Microsoft Internet Explorer and has the ActiveX Control for Shockwave already installed, it will recognize the *EMBED* tag. Unfortunately, if it's not installed, MSIE will not recognize the tag. For these users, the *OBJECT* tag must be used. Unfortunately Netscape doesn't recognize the *OBJECT* tag. Thankfully, there is a cross-browser solution to this problem, as seen in the template shown in Figure A-3.

The *OBJECT* tag contains the same type of information as the *EMBED* tag shown earlier, but is arranged somewhat differently:

- The *CLASSID* parameter is the identifier for the Shockwave ActiveX Control.
- The *CODEBASE* parameter contains the URL of the ActiveX Control, so MSIE can get it if the user doesn't already have it installed.
- The *WIDTH* and *HEIGHT* parameters work the same as with the *EMBED* tag.
- The *NAME* parameter allows the object to be used within a *FORM* block and to be included in the submit process.
- The *ID* parameter is a document-wide identifier that can be used as a destination of a hypertext link.

Template for cross-browser integration of Shockwave in HTML

```
<HTML>
<HEAD>
<TITLE>
Title this page
</TITLE>
</HEAD>
<BODY>
<OBJECT CLASSID="clsid:166B1BCA-3F9C-11CF-8075-444553540000"
CODEBASE="http://active.macromedia.com/director/cabs/sw.cab#version=5,0,1,61"
WIDTH="300" HEIGHT="300" NAME="Shockwave"
ID="swmovie1">
<PARAM NAME="SRC" VALUE="http://webreview.com/shockwave.dcr">
<PARAM NAME="BGCOLOR" VALUE="#000000">
<PARAM NAME="PALETTE" VALUE="foreground">
<EMBED SRC=http://webreview.com/shockwave.dcr HEIGHT=300 WIDTH=300
PALETTE=foreground BGCOLOR=#000000
PLUGINSPAGE=http://www.macromedia.com/shockwave>
</OBJECT>
</BODY>
</HTML>
```

Figure A-3.

Additional parameters identify the URL of the Shockwave movie *(SRC)*, the *BGCOLOR* of the movie's background and the *PALETTE* to use. These parameters work the same as their *EMBED* counterparts. (For more on Microsoft Internet Explorer and external parameters see the sidebar, "ActiveX and external parameters.")

Step three: Uploading to your server

The next step is to upload your Shockwave movie to your server as you would any other graphic or sound file. Macintosh users should choose the *Raw Data* option when uploading a Shockwave movie via Fetch.

Step four: Configuring your server

Anytime you want to use a server to deliver content of a different MIME type, you must first configure your server to do so. A MIME type is so named because it is an acronym for Multiple Internet Mail Extensions. Originally MIMEs where created to extend the capabilities of email and they soon became a standard

ActiveX and external parameters

The *OBJECT* tag used with the ActiveX Control only supports certain predefined parameters and ignores all others, as opposed to the Netscape plug-in, which accepts any user-defined parameter. In addition to the *SRC, BGCOLOR,* and *PALETTE* parameters, the *OBJECT* tag also accepts these parameters (use the syntax < PARAM NAME = "name" VALUE = "value" >):

Name	Value
swURL	URL for other Shockwave movie or SWA file
swText	Specify text to be used in the Shockwave movie
swForeColor	Specify the foreground color of an object in the movie
swBackColor	Specify the background color of an object in the movie
swFrame	Specify a target frame in a URL
swColor	Specify the color of an object in the movie
swName	Specify a user name for use in the movie
swPassword	Specify a user password for use in the movie
swBanner	Specify text for use as a banner in the movie
swSound	Specify a sound to be played or turn sound on or off
swVolume	Specify the sound volume for a movie
swPreLoadTime	Specify the preload time of an SWA file
swAudio	Specify the URL of an audio file to play in the movie
swList	Specify list of items to be used in the movie
sw1–9	Additional parameters for author-defined use

for the Web as well. A MIME basically tells the server three things about the content you are serving: the type of data, the creator of the data, and the file extensions of the data. Without this information the server does not know what data you are serving and an error will result.

Shockwave is such a popular format nowadays that most Internet Service Providers (ISPs) have already configured their servers to serve Shockwave movies. If yours hasn't, or if your company operates their own server, you need to give your System Administer three bits of information about the Shockwave MIME type:

- Type: application
- Creator: x-director
- File extensions: .dir, .dxr, and .dcr (.dcr being most important)

If you need further information on configuring your specific server, Macromedia's Web site contains all the information you or your system administrator will need to configure UNIX, Mac, and NT servers. This information is available at *http://www. macromedia.com/shockwave/ config.html#server.*

If your ISP uses a UNIX server, it may also be possible for you to add the necessary MIME type to your public directory, without the assistance of the system administrator. To do this, follow these steps:

First, in any word processing program create a new file. In this file type the following three lines:

```
AddType application/x-director dcr
AddType application/x-director dir
AddType application/x-director dxr
```

Next, save this file and name it *.htaccess* (be sure to put the period in front of the name). Upload this file to the public level of your directory on your server. For example, if you have a URL of *http://www.some_server.com/ ~bschmitt,* in the *bschmitt* directory there will typically be a directory called *public_html.* This is where you want to place the *.htaccess* file. Not *in* the public folder, but at the same level as the public folder. When a browser requests your Shockwave movies from your server, this file will be read by the server and give it the information it needs to know about Shockwave.

Step five: Test, test, test

As with any project, the last step is to test to be sure everything is working. Be certain to test using several different browsers on several different platforms and at various monitor bit depths to ensure that the world is seeing what you intended.

B Net-Specific Extensions to Lingo

The Lingo authoring language has been extended specifically for use with Shockwave and the Internet. Unfortunately, Net-specific Lingo, at the time of this writing, is understood only by the Shockwave plug-in and ActiveX Control, but not by Director itself, which can make testing inconvenient. Here is a quick reference of Net-specific Lingo commands and functions. For more information on how to use individual commands see Chapter 9, *Using Net-Specific Lingo.*

For additional information on Net-specific Lingo, see the Developer's reference on Macromedia's site at *http://www.macromedia.com/ shockwave/developer.html.*

getNetText "*URL***"** — This command retrieves the text from the file located at the URL specified. This command can also be used to pass variables to a CGI script and retrieve the result from the CGI script back into Shockwave. To pass variables to a CGI script use the syntax:

> getNetText "http://your_server/your_cgi_bin/your_cgi? variable1=value1&variable2=value2&etc"

netTextResult( ) — Use this function to capture the text retrieved with the *getNetText* command. This command puts the retrieved text into a field or variable.

preLoadNetThing "*URL***"** — This command loads something from the Net into the browser's cache. It only loads the thing specified. If you load an HTML page from the Web, it will preload just the HTML of the page, not all the images and movies on the page. For each of those you must issue separate *preLoadNetThing* commands. Use this command to preload items that you will use later, so the user won't have to wait for downloading.

gotoNetMovie "URL" — This command retrieves the movie at the URL specified and plays it in place of the movie it is called from. If more than one *gotoNetMovie* command is issued, the subsequent commands cancel out the previous ones.

gotoNetPage "URL", "optional-target frame" — This command retrieves the Net page at the URL specified and loads it into the target frame specified (if any). Any custom-named frame can be targeted, as well as any of Netscape's special reserved target names such as: *_blank, _self, _parent,* and *_top.*

netAbort — This command immediately aborts an asynchronous Net operation.

netDone( ) — This function checks if an asynchronous Net operation — such as *getNetText, preLoadNetThing,* or *gotoNetPage* — has been completed. This command returns *true* if the operation is completed and *false* if it is still in progress.

netError( ) — This function returns a string when the most recent Net operation is done. If the operation was successful, it returns *ok.* If the operation fails, it returns a string describing the error.

netMIME( ) — This function returns the MIME type of an item retrieved through an asynchronous Net operation.

netLastModDate( ) — This function returns a string with the date last modified from the header of the item retrieved through an asynchronous Net operation.

getLatestNetID( ) — This function returns a unique identifier for the asynchronous Net operation.

netStatus "message" — This command allows you to place a message in the status area of a Net browser. One very good use for this is to place a copyright notice in your file. That way, if someone uses your .dcr file on their site, your copyright notice will be indelibly burned into the file.

setPref *filename, filevalue* — This command writes to a folder named *prefs* in the Shockwave Director plug-in support folder. You must name the file you wish to write to and the string you wish to write. If the pref file does not already exist in the *prefs* folder, it is created.

getPref*(filename)* — This function retrieves the contents of a file that was previously written with the *setPref* command.

externalParamCount*(n)* — Function that returns the number of external parameters that are passed to the Shockwave movie from the *EMBED* or *OBJECT* tags in the HTML document.

externalParamName*(n)* — Function that returns the names of external parameters that are passed to the Shockwave movie from the *EMBED* or *OBJECT* tags in the HTML document.

externalParamValue*(n)* — Function that returns the values contained in external parameters that are passed to the Shockwave movie from the *EMBED* or *OBJECT* tags in the HTML document. If *n* is a number, the value contained in the *nth* position of the list of parameters will be returned. If *n* is a string, the value contained in the parameter that matches the string will be returned. Strings are case-sensitive, so they must match exactly.

Lingo for Shockwave Audio

For additional information on Lingo for audio, see Chapter 11.

URL — Property that sets the URL for the location of a SWA file on the Internet.

preLoadTime — Property that sets the amount of audio data to be preloaded before play begins. This amount is measured in seconds. Keep in mind, the number of seconds set doesn't refer to the amount of time it takes to download the data, but rather the amount of data itself. Depending on the speed of the users connection, the time it takes to download this data will vary.

preLoadBuffer (member, "SWA file") — Command that begins the preloading of the amount of data set by the *preLoadTime* property.

play (member, "SWA file") — Command that begins play of an SWA file.

stop (member, "SWA file") — Command that stops play of an SWA file.

pause (member, "SWA file") — Command that pauses play of an SWA file.

the state of member "SWA file" — Property that returns the state of the SWA file. Returns a numerical code for the various states:

0	stopped
1	preloading
2	preload done
3	playing
4	paused
5	done
9	error

the duration of member "SWA file" — Property that returns the duration in seconds of the SWA file.

the percentStreamed of member "SWA file" — Property that returns the percent of the SWA file that has been streamed.

the percentPlayed of member "SWA file" — Property that returns the percent of the SWA file that has been played.

the bitRate of member "SWA file" — Property that returns the bit rate of the SWA file that has been preloaded.

getError(member "SWA file") and **getErrorString(member "SWA file")** — Functions that return the error information about the SWA file.

Errors returned by these functions are:

getError returns:	*getErrorString* returns:
0	OK
1	memory
2	network
3	playback device
99	other

Lingo disabled in Shockwave

If you're having trouble making a Lingo command work in Shockwave that you've always had success with in your other Director projects, it may be because the command has been disabled. For reasons of security — preventing the ability to create a hostile Shockwave movie that could harm a user's computer — and for reasons related to the difficulties of data transmission over the Internet, Macromedia has disabled certain Director functions found in Director for use with Shockwave. For your reference, here is the list of currently disabled Lingo commands:

closeDA	openResFile
closeResFile	open window
close window	openXLib
closeXLib	pasteFromClipboard
fileIO	pathName
fileName of cast	printFrom
fileName of window	quit
getNthFileNameInFolder	restart
importFileInto	saveMovie
mci	searchCurrentFolder
moviePath	searchPaths
open	serialIO
openDA	shutdown

In addition to these commands Shockwave movies cannot use movie-in-a-window, custom menus, or any of the wait settings in the tempo channel. Also, although Shockwave can use linked media — such as external casts, QuickTime, and AVI movies — as well as Xtras and Xobjects, they must be present in the user's Shockwave support folder inside their browser's plug-ins folder. These items may be delivered via separate download or through disk, but must be installed in their proper place by the user, which makes them all the more difficult to justify using.

Director and Shockwave Resources on the Web

For updates and additions to this list, see the companion Web site to this book at *http://webreview.com/ books/shockwave/*.

Castle Productions

http://www.best.com/~mcastle/

Contains a good-sized list of downloadable Lingo script examples. Lots of stuff to learn here.

Clever Media

http://clevermedia.com/

Includes a Lingo and Shockwave tip of the week, plus several Clever Tool Xtras for Director. Also check out the Clever Media Shockwave arcade of games.

Click Zone

http://www.ddce.cqu.edu.au/imu/tools/Director/home.html

A small collection of XObjects, Xtras, Lingo scripts, and Shockwave movies to peruse.

Director Web

http://hakatai.mcli.dist.maricopa.edu/director/index.html

For more information see "Maricop-A-Sketch and the Director Web" on page 73.

Dirigo Multimedia

http://www.maine.com/shops/gpicher/

Freelance Multimedia developer Glenn Picher offers an ever expanding collection of useful Xtras for Director.

Dr. Lingo

http://www.zeek.com/drlingo.html

Email your toughest Lingo questions to Dr. Lingo and he'll mail you back the answer. Also available are downloadable Lingo script samples from the members of the *Strictly Lingo* Director SIG (special interest group) of Los Angeles.

Fusion

http://www.conknet.com/~d_abad/fusion/FUSION.HTMLX
An online magazine for interactive media and graphics arts professionals and wanna-bes. Occasionally covers Director and Shockwave issues.

G/Matter, Inc.

http://www.gmatter.com/
Publishers of resources and Xtras for Director. Including the MediaBook CD, Director ToolBox Pro, Killer Transitions, and PopMenu, Sound, Print-O-Matic, and Trans-X Xtras. Site includes online ordering information.

Integration New Media

http://www.integration.qc.ca/
Developers of the V12 Database Engine Xtra for Director.

Lingo User's Journal

http://www.penworks.com/LUJ/home.html
Online ordering of the LUJ newsletter, a monthly newsletter devoted to Lingo. View the contents of back issues and order online. You can also view a sample issue in PDF format and download source code samples of Lingo from recent issues of LUJ.

Macromedia

http://www.macromedia.com/
Macromedia's own Web site. Includes lots of product info as well as a valuable Shockwave Developer's Center that contains a wealth of information on getting started with Shockwave. Also includes several galleries of shocked sites and a "Shocked Site of the Day." Site includes online ordering of Macromedia products.

The Marc Canter Show

http://mediaband.com/
This site contains a veritable feast of eye candy from the man who invented Director, Marc Canter. Meet Marc and all his friends as you explore this site full of vivid and dynamic Shocked content.

Media Lab

http://www.medialab.com/software/

Makers of several valuable Xtras, including PhotoCaster, which allows direct import of Photoshop layers into Director.

MpegXtra

http://www.tbaiana.com/ing/mpegx/menmpg.htm

Information about a Director Xtra for incorporating full-screen MPEG compressed videos.

Newsgroup

alt.multimedia.director

Newgroup for discussion of a variety of Director topics.

Nine Trees Design

http://www.pacific.net/~david/ntd/ntd_director.html

Freeware and shareware Director Lingo solutions.

Pete's size and compression tips

http://www.etrc.ox.ac.uk/personal/pr/sizetips.html

Peter Robinson offers his tips online.

Project Multimedia

http://www.project.com/project/matts/director.html

An engagingly written beginner's guide to Director.

Red Eye Software

http://www.halcyon.com/redeye/

Developers of XObjects and Xtras for use with Director. Site includes some technical tips for XObject development.

Shared Cast ftp site

ftp://sharedcast.hccs.cc.tx.us/Director/

This ftp site has lots of Director-related stuff to download. Included are lots of cool programs, Lingo scripts, Xtras and samples from the members of the Direct-L mailing list.

Shared Cast Direct-L Scripting Examples

http://sharedcast.hccs.cc.tx.us/directL.html

A collection of downloadable Lingo scripts from the members of the Direct-L mailing list.

ShockeR

http://www.shocker.com/

This is the Web site for the ShockeR Mailing List, a listserv email list dedicated to the discussion of Shockwave development. This list is rapidly becoming one of the very best sources for Shockwave information available. Along with instructions on how to subscribe to the list, there is also a searchable digest of archived list discussions, a Shockwave FAQ (frequently asked questions), an alphabetized list of Shocked sites on the Web, and the Cool ShockeR Site — a cool new shocked site chosen each week.

Shockwave Baubles

http://www.adveract.com/abtboble.htm

A collection of free Shockwave movies available for download all under 12K. The site also includes tips for creating those really small movies.

Smoke and Mirrors Tech Notes

http://mediaband.com/mediaband/collins/technotes.html

Some very good tutorials on Shockwave and Director from developer Jim Collins.

SpriteLib Central

http://www.walrus.com/~ari/spritlib.htm

This site offers a nifty selection of professionally drawn sprites for game animations. They're all free and the only caveats for usage is that you register with the owner and give him credit.

Update Stage

http://www.updatestage.com/

A collection of Director techniques, quirks and bugs gathered from the author's personal experiences in Director development.

Xtra Media

http://www.xtramedia.com/

Developers of Xtras and Xobjects for use with Director. Site also has a small Lingo Tips section in a Q&A format.

D
What's on the CD?

There is much more to explore in the many examples in this book than I've been able to describe in the available space — this is why I've included the source Director files of nearly all the examples discussed in the book, and several that aren't mentioned at all.

The samples in this book and on the CD are to be used by way of example only. They are intended to instruct and inspire you to create your own projects. The art contained in each movie remains the exclusive property of their creators. It is not clip art, and should not be treated as such.

Following is a list of the folders on the disc and their contents:

Source folder

The *source* folder includes the source Director files listed below. To view these movies, simply double-click them and the save-disabled version of Director, included on the disc, will automatically launch.

cajones.dir	hangman.dir	orbiter.dir	window.dir
carver.dir	icons.dir	raspbery.dir	winter.dir
doodle.dir	maze.dir	shock.dir	
doodle2.dir	miracle.dir	sketch.dir	
door.dir	odradio.dir	tsm.dir	

Samples folder

The *samples* folder contains the Jazzman game and an updated version of the multi maze (in a folder called *WWMaze*) described in Chapter 9. Also included in *samples* are *palette.pic* and *palette.dir* as described on page 114.

Tutorial folder

The *tutorial* folder contains the files for use with the animation tutorial in Chapter 2. The *cast* folder contains the nine PICT files for import into Director and the *source* folder contains the four Director files as described in the tutorial.

Software folder (Macintosh)

The *software* folder contains three folders, *Director Demo, Sound Edit 16 v2,* and *Shockwave Essentials.*

Director Demo

The *Director Demo* folder contains a fully-featured (save-disabled) copy of Macromedia Director. To launch Director, double-click the *Director 5* icon in the folder *Director 5 - Save Disabled.* The *Director 5 - Installer* folder contains the installer for the save-disabled version, for installation on your hard drive. The installer will also install QuickTime 2.1 and Sound Manager 3.1 if you don't already have them.

Sound Edit 16 v2

To install a save-disabled demo of Sound Edit 16, double-click on the *SoundEdit 16 version 2 Demo* icon.

Shockwave Essentials

To install the Shockwave plug-in for Netscape or Microsoft Internet Explorer, double-click the *SWEssentials 68K Installer* icon for non-PowerPC Macs, or the *SWEssentials PPC Installer* icon for PowerPC models.

Software folder (Windows)

The *software* folder contains two folders, *Dirwin* and *Shockwin.*

Dirwin

The *Dirwin* folder contains an installer for a save-disabled version of Macromedia Director 5. To install Director, run *setup.exe* and follow the installer instructions.

Shockwin

To install the Shockwave plug-in for Netscape, run *n16e0001.exe* for Windows 3.1 or *n32e0001.exe* for Windows 95.

Index

More Titles from O'REILLY™

Web Publishing

GIF Animation Studio: Animating Your Web Site

By Richard Koman
1st Edition November 1996
180 pages, Includes CD-ROM
ISBN 1-56592-230-1

 GIF animation is bringing the Web to life — without plug-ins, Java programming or expensive authoring programs. This book profiles the major GIF animation programs, profiles work by leading designers (including John Hersey, Razorfish, Henrik Drescher, and Erik Josowitz), and documents advanced animation techniques. *GIF Animation Studio* is the first release in the new Web Review Studio series.

The Web Studio series — published by O'Reilly & Associates' affiliate company, Songline Studios, publishers of the groundbreaking Web sites Web Review and Ferndale — demystifies the complexities of publishing multimedia on the Web. The series is aimed at creative Web professionals and enthusiasts — the people creating graphics, animation, sound, and multimedia on the Web.

HTML: The Definitive Guide

By Chuck Musciano & Bill Kennedy
2nd Edition Winter 1997
420 pages (est.), ISBN 1-56592-175-5

 *HTML: The Definitive Guide*, second edition, is a complete guide to creating documents on the World Wide Web. This book describes basic syntax and semantics and goes on to show you how to create beautiful, informative, and dynamic Web documents you'll be proud to display.

The second edition covers the most up-to-date version of the HTML standard (the proposed HTML version 3.2), Netscape 3.0 and Internet Explorer 3.0, plus all the common extensions, especially Netscape extensions. The authors cover each and every element of the currently accepted version of the language in detail, explaining how each element works and how it interacts with all the other elements. They've also included a style guide that helps you decide how to best use HTML to accomplish a variety of tasks, from simple online documentation to complex marketing and sales presentations. Readers of the first edition can find the updates for the second edition on the Web at *www.ora.com*.

Designing for the Web: Getting Started in a New Medium

By Jennifer Niederst with Edie Freedman
1st Edition April 1996
180 pages, ISBN 1-56592-165-8

 *Designing for the Web* gives you the basics you need to hit the ground running. Although geared toward designers, it covers information and techniques useful to anyone who wants to put graphics online. It explains how to work with HTML documents from a designer's point of view, outlines special problems with presenting information online, and walks through incorporating images into Web pages, with emphasis on resolution and improving efficiency.

JavaScript: The Definitive Guide

By David Flanagan
1st Edition Winter 1997
700 pages (est.), ISBN 1-56592-234-4

 This definitive reference guide to JavaScript, the HTML extension that gives Web pages programming language capa-bilities, covers JavaScript as it is used in Netscape 3.0 and 2.0 and in Microsoft Internet Explorer 2.0. Learn how JavaScript really works (and when it doesn't). Use JavaScript to control Web browser behavior, add dynamically created text to Web pages, interact with users through HTML forms, and even control and interact with Java applets and Navigator plug-ins.

Building Your Own WebSite

By Susan B. Peck & Stephen Arrants
1st Edition July 1996
514 pages, ISBN 1-56592-232-8

 A hands-on reference for Windows® 95 and Windows NT™ desktop users who want to host their own site on the Web or on a corporate intranet. This step-by-step guide will have you creating live Web pages in minutes. You'll also learn how to connect your web to information in other Windows applications, such as word processing documents and databases. Packed with examples and tutorials on every aspect of Web management. Includes highly acclaimed WebSite™ 1.1—all the software you need for Web publishing.

For information: **800-998-9938**, *707-829-0515;* **info@ora.com; http://www.ora.com/**
To order: **800-889-8969** *(credit card orders only);* **order@ora.com**

Stay in touch with O'REILLY™

Visit Our Award-Winning World Wide Web Site

http://www.ora.com/

VOTED

"Top 100 Sites on the Web" —*PC Magazine*
"Top 5% Websites" —*Point Communications*
"3-Star site" —*The McKinley Group*

Our Web site contains a library of comprehensive product information (including book excerpts and tables of contents), downloadable software, background articles, interviews with technology leaders, links to relevant sites, book cover art, and more. File us in your Bookmarks or Hotlist!

Join Our Two Email Mailing Lists

LIST #1   NEW PRODUCT RELEASES: To receive automatic email with brief descriptions of all new O'Reilly products as they are released, send email to: listproc@online.ora.com and put the following information in the first line of your message (NOT in the Subject: field, which is ignored): **subscribe ora-news "Your Name" of "Your Organization"** (for example: **subscribe ora-news Kris Webber of Fine Enterprises)**

List #2   O'REILLY EVENTS: If you'd also like us to send information about trade show events, special promotions, and other O'Reilly events, send email to: **listproc@online.ora.com** and put the following information in the first line of your message (NOT in the Subject: field, which is ignored): **subscribe ora-events "Your Name" of "Your Organization"**

Visit Our Gopher Site

• Connect your Gopher to **gopher.ora.com**, or
• Point your Web browser to **gopher://gopher.ora.com/**, or
• telnet to **gopher.ora.com** (login: **gopher**)

Get Example Files from Our Books Via FTP

There are two ways to access an archive of example files from our books:

REGULAR FTP — ftp to: **ftp.ora.com** (login: **anonymous**—use your email address as the password) or point your Web browser to: **ftp://ftp.ora.com/**

FTPMAIL — Send an email message to: **ftpmail@online.ora.com** (write "help" in the message body)

Contact Us Via Email

order@ora.com — To place a book or software order online. Good for North American and international customers.

subscriptions@ora.com — To place an order for any of our newsletters or periodicals.

software@ora.com — For general questions and product information about our software.
  • Check out O'Reilly Software Online at **http://software.ora.com/** for software and technical support information.
  • Registered O'Reilly software users send your questions to **website-support@ora.com**

books@ora.com — For General questions about any of our books.

cs@ora.com — For solutions to problems regarding your order or our products.

booktech@ora.com — For book content technical questions or corrections.

proposals@ora.com — To submit book or software proposals to our editors and product managers.

international@ora.com — For information about our international distributors or translation queries.
  • For a list of our distributors outside of North America check out: **http://www.ora.com/www/order/country.html**

O'REILLY™

101 Morris Street, Sebastopol, CA 95472 USA
TEL 707-829-0515 or 800-998-9938 (6 A.M. to 5 P.M. PST)
FAX 707-829-0104

These Guys Want To Be Shocked.

Macromedia Shockwave™

Here's Everything You Need To Do It.

Create and deliver electrifying education materials, from print to the Web.

Today's kids brag about baud rates. They work on new Pentiums or Power PCs instead of old Pontiacs. And they quote lines from Wired™ instead of Whitman.

Tough crowd.

But they're all yours if you have the Macromedia® Studios with Shockwave™. Products that help you create the hottest multimedia courseware and deliver it across campus or around the world.

You see, there's only one family of software for graphics and multimedia on the Internet. There's only one set of tools that helps you create everything from 2D to 3D to full-blown Web sites. There's only one name you need to know. Macromedia.

Take Authorware®, the educator's choice for interactive courseware and training— which now helps you create materials to be sent streaming across your intranet. Or the Director® Multimedia Studio,™ which sets the industry standard in multimedia. For illustration, page layout, font creation, hi-res image editing and 3D modeling, pick up the FreeHand™ Graphics Studio.™ And the Backstage™ Desktop Studio lets you create powerful database-driven Web sites, with no programming or scripting required.

To top it off, we're introducing electronic documentation versions of Director and the FreeHand Graphics Studio. Just another way Macromedia makes multimedia and graphics affordable for both educators AND students.

So here's your assignment: see for yourself how Macromedia can electrify your course-ware and shock any audience. Call for our free brochure, "Macromedia in Education: 12 Case Studies," as well as the latest Showcase™ CD. Then take advantage of our new low education prices—just $649 for Authorware, $249 for the FreeHand Graphics Studio, and $299 for Director. And of course, don't miss our Web site.

The Macromedia Studios and Shockwave. Because when it comes to cutting-edge courseware, shock value is everything.

Call 1-800-220-5978
http://www.macromedia.com/

MACROMEDIA®
Tools To Power Your Ideas™

Songline Studios, Inc. End-User License Agreement

Here's a page we encourage readers to tear out...

The Web Review Studio series

This new series from O'Reilly & Associates and Songline Studios, demystifies the complexities of publishing on the Web. Unlike other Web books, Web Review Studio books don't just tell you how to create Web content; we show you how leading designers are implementing technology for compelling communication. Upcoming books will cover JavaScript, streaming audio, navigation design and more.

TELL ME ABOUT UPCOMING STUDIO BOOKS

Thank you for purchasing *Shockwave Studio*

Where did you buy this book?
❏ Bookstore
❏ Tradeshow
❏ Direct from O'Reilly
❏ Online
❏ Class/Seminar
❏ Other _____

What operating system do you use?
❏ Macintosh
❏ Windows NT
❏ Windows 95
❏ Other _____

What is your job description?
❏ Designer/Art Director
❏ WebMaster/Developer
❏ Marketing Communications
❏ Other _____

What other Web development topics interest you?
❏ Java/JavaScript
❏ HTML
❏ Audio
❏ ActiveX
❏ Video
❏ Web Design
❏ Other _____

Name _____ Company/Organization _____

Address _____

City _____ State _____ Zip/Postal Code _____ Country _____

Telephone _____ Internet or other email address (specify network) _____

Songline Studios specializes in developing innovative, interactive content for online audiences. Visit the many online and print properties created by Songline Studios through their Website located at http://www.songline.com

POST CARD

Songline Inc., 101 Morris Street, Sebastopol, CA 95472-9902

BUSINESS REPLY MAIL
FIRST CLASS MAIL   PERMIT NO. 80   SEBASTOPOL, CA

Postage will be paid by addressee

O'Reilly & Associates, Inc.
101 Morris Street
Sebastopol, CA 95472-9902